Barbara Rae
Arctic Sketchbook

Royal Academy of Arts

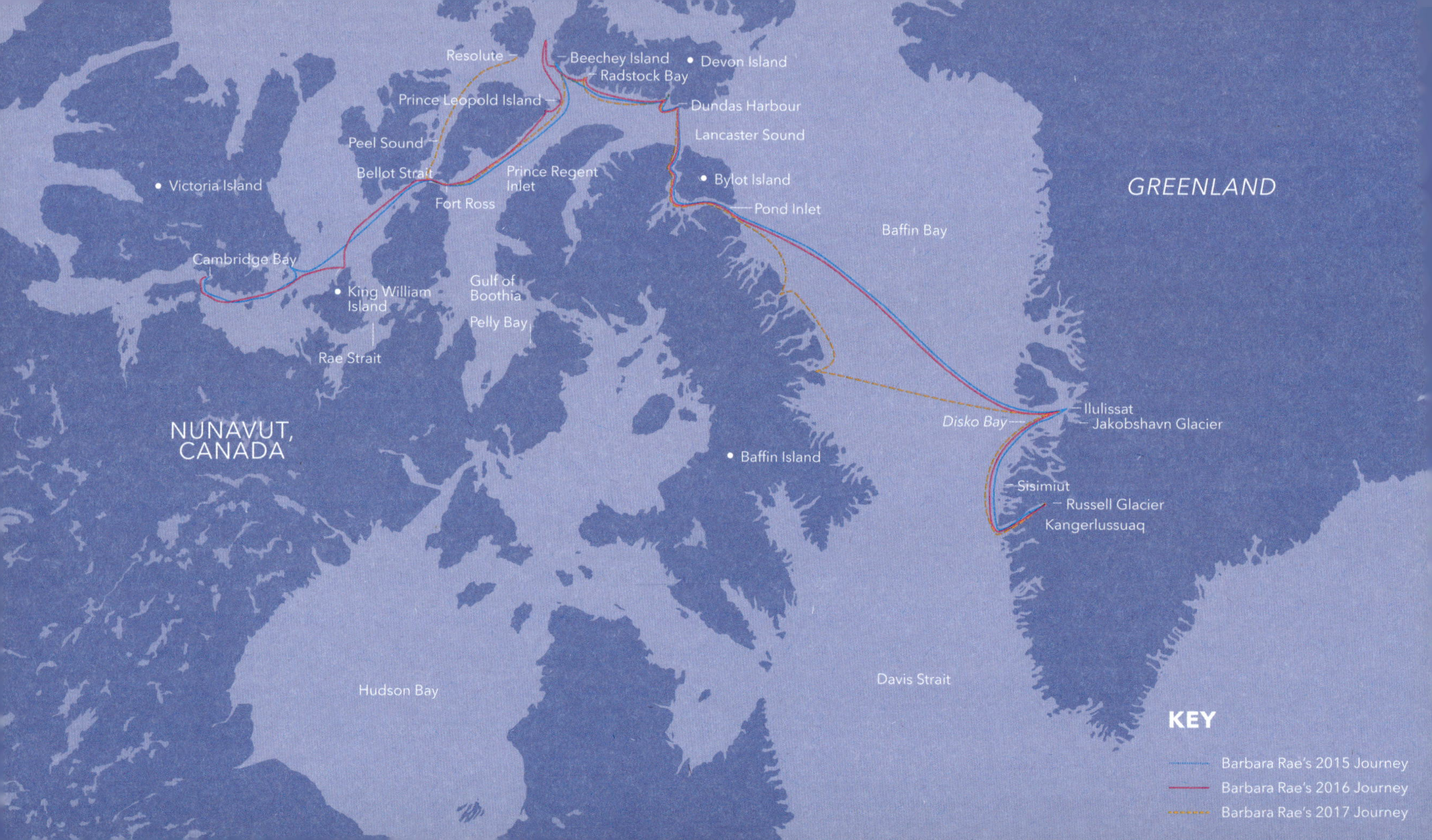
Resolute
Beechey Island
Devon Island
Radstock Bay
Prince Leopold Island
Dundas Harbour
Lancaster Sound
Peel Sound
Bellot Strait
Prince Regent Inlet
Victoria Island
Fort Ross
Bylot Island
Pond Inlet
GREENLAND
Baffin Bay
Cambridge Bay
King William Island
Gulf of Boothia
Pelly Bay
Rae Strait
Ilulissat
Disko Bay
Jakobshavn Glacier
NUNAVUT, CANADA
Baffin Island
Sisimiut
Russell Glacier
Kangerlussuaq
Hudson Bay
Davis Strait
KEY
Barbara Rae's 2015 Journey
Barbara Rae's 2016 Journey
Barbara Rae's 2017 Journey

Greenland and NW Passage Aug 2015

Aug 11
Leave Ottawa
to Kangerlussuaq
Airport
Desolate Settlement
built round
Old US AirBase
Boarded Vavilov
sail down
Sondre Strøm
Fjord. and
exit fjord in
morning to
Davis Strait

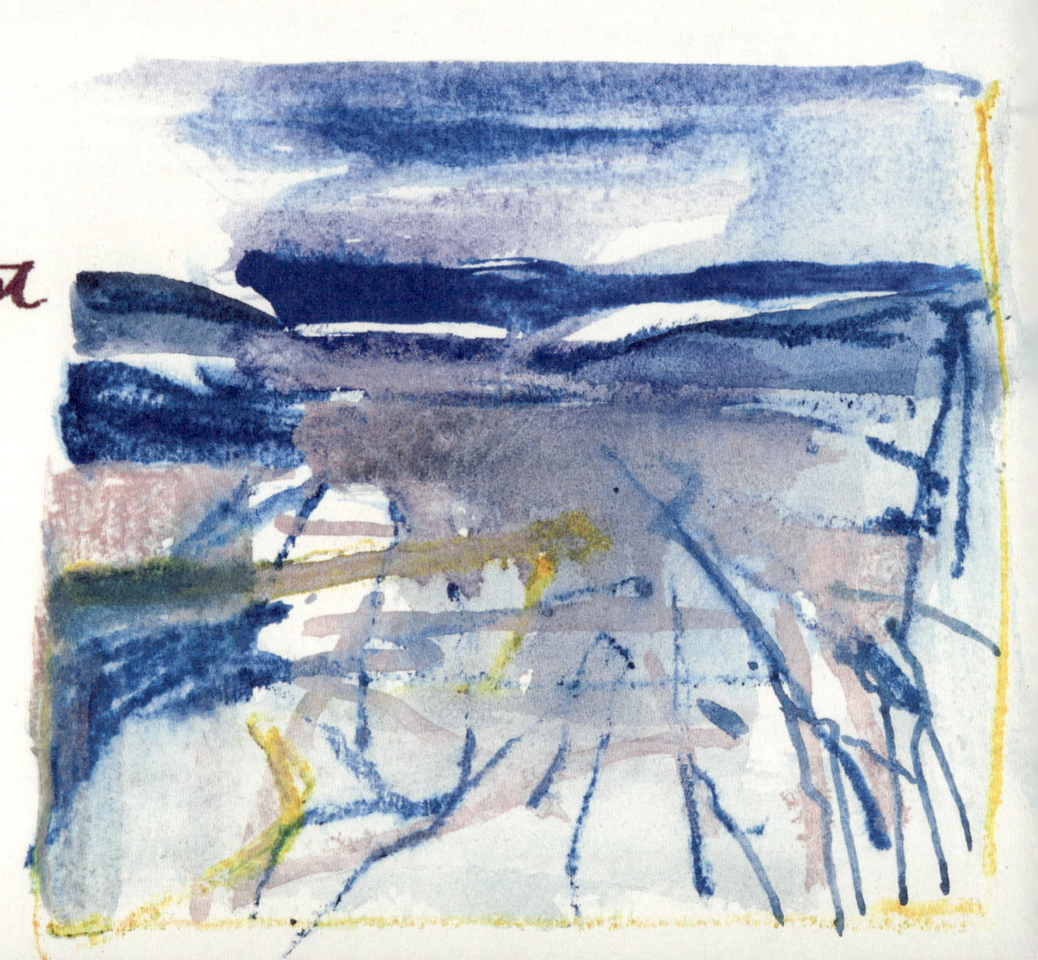

aug 12
arrive in
Sissimiut
harbour.
look round
village, go
to museum
a random
collection
of coloured
houses.
Whaling
harbour.
Bored huskys

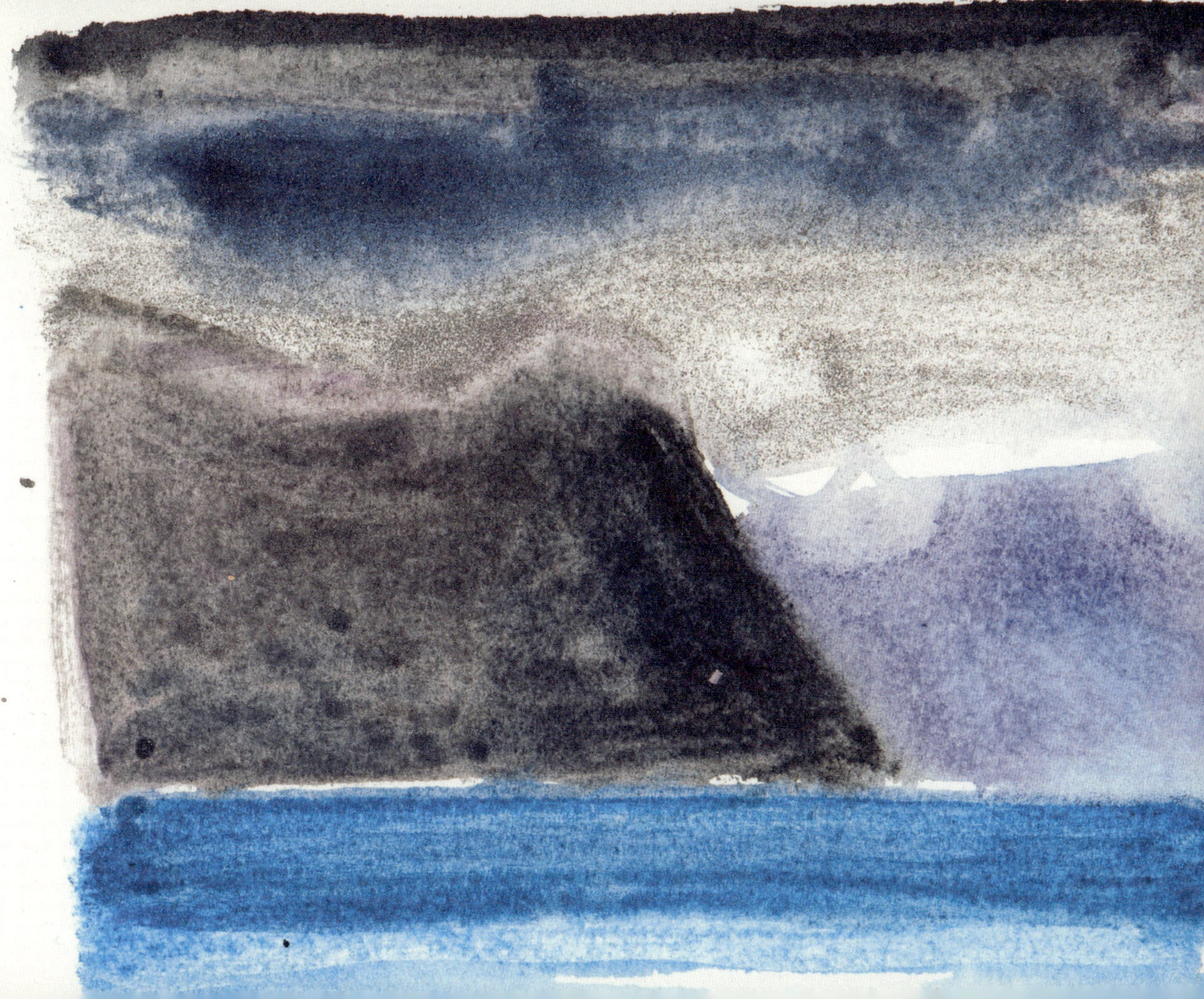

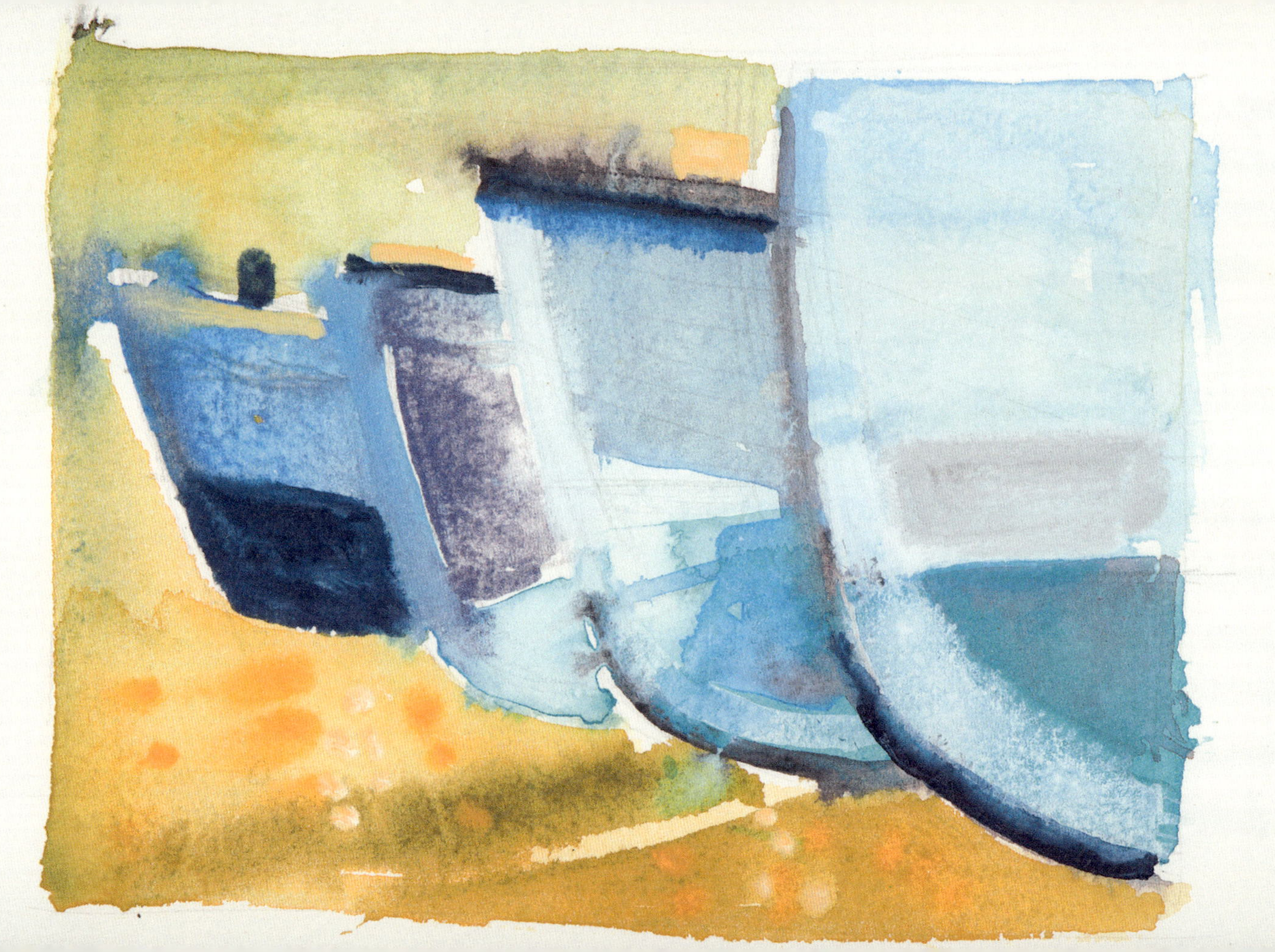

Aug 13
Overnight sail
from Sisimiut
to Illulissat.
Setting sun
does not set.
Flat calm Davis
Straight.

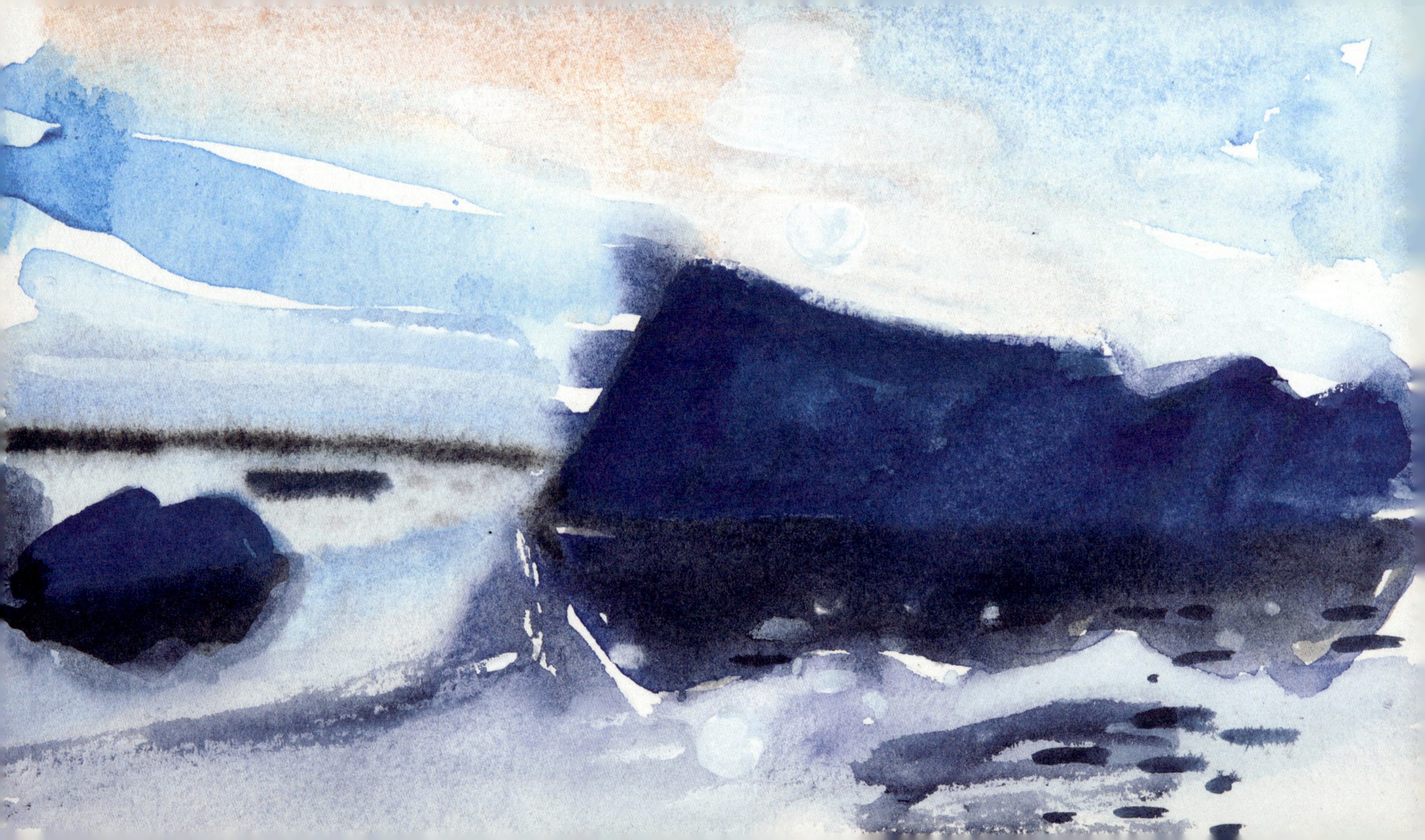

Aug 14
Sail from
Sissimiut to
Illulissat,
Disko Bay
Surrounded
by Icebergs
large + small
Wonderful
Sunny warm
day. Go by
Zodiac to tour
Icebergs.
Afternoon try to
reach Illulissat
by Zodiac but
ice too dense
out for three
hours.

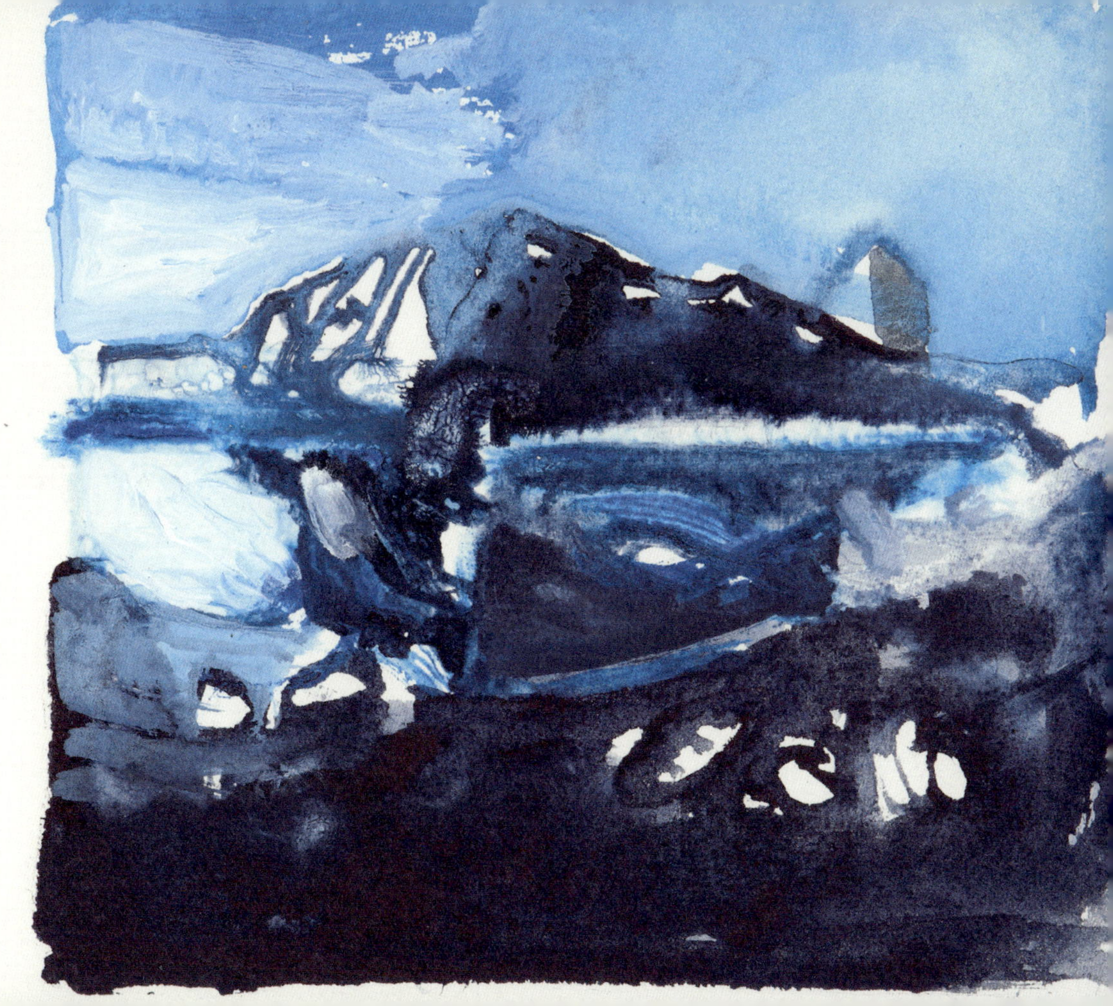

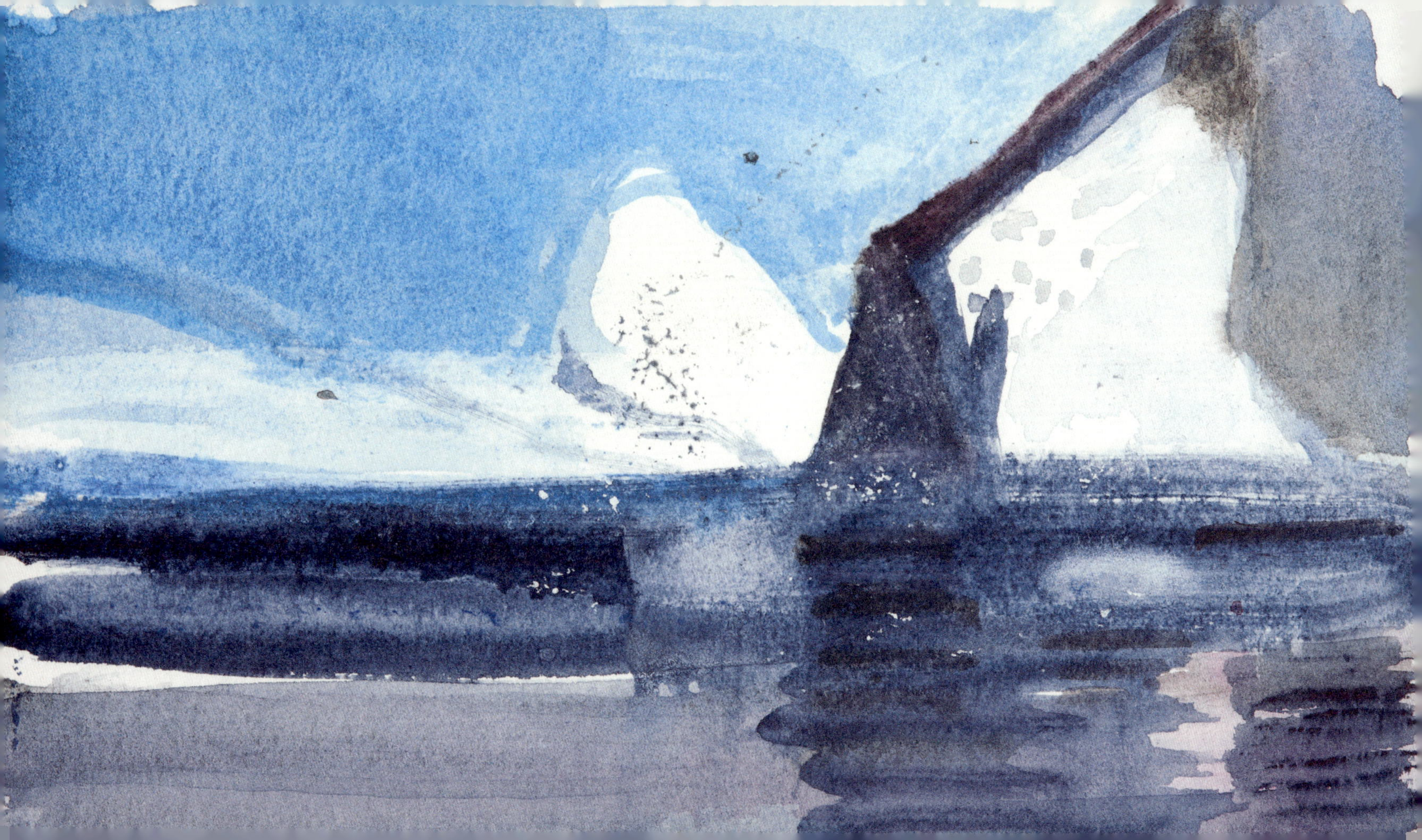

Aug 14
Cruise round
Icebergs.
in Disko Bay
leave for
Baffin Bay

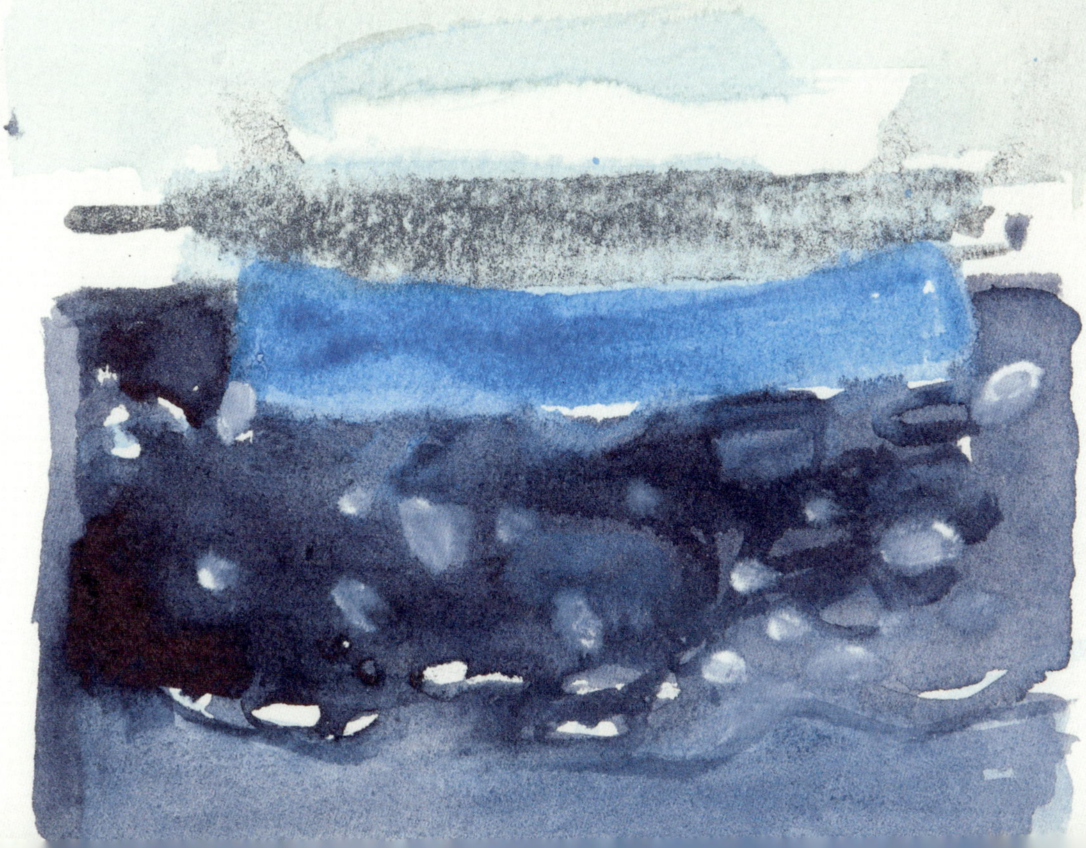

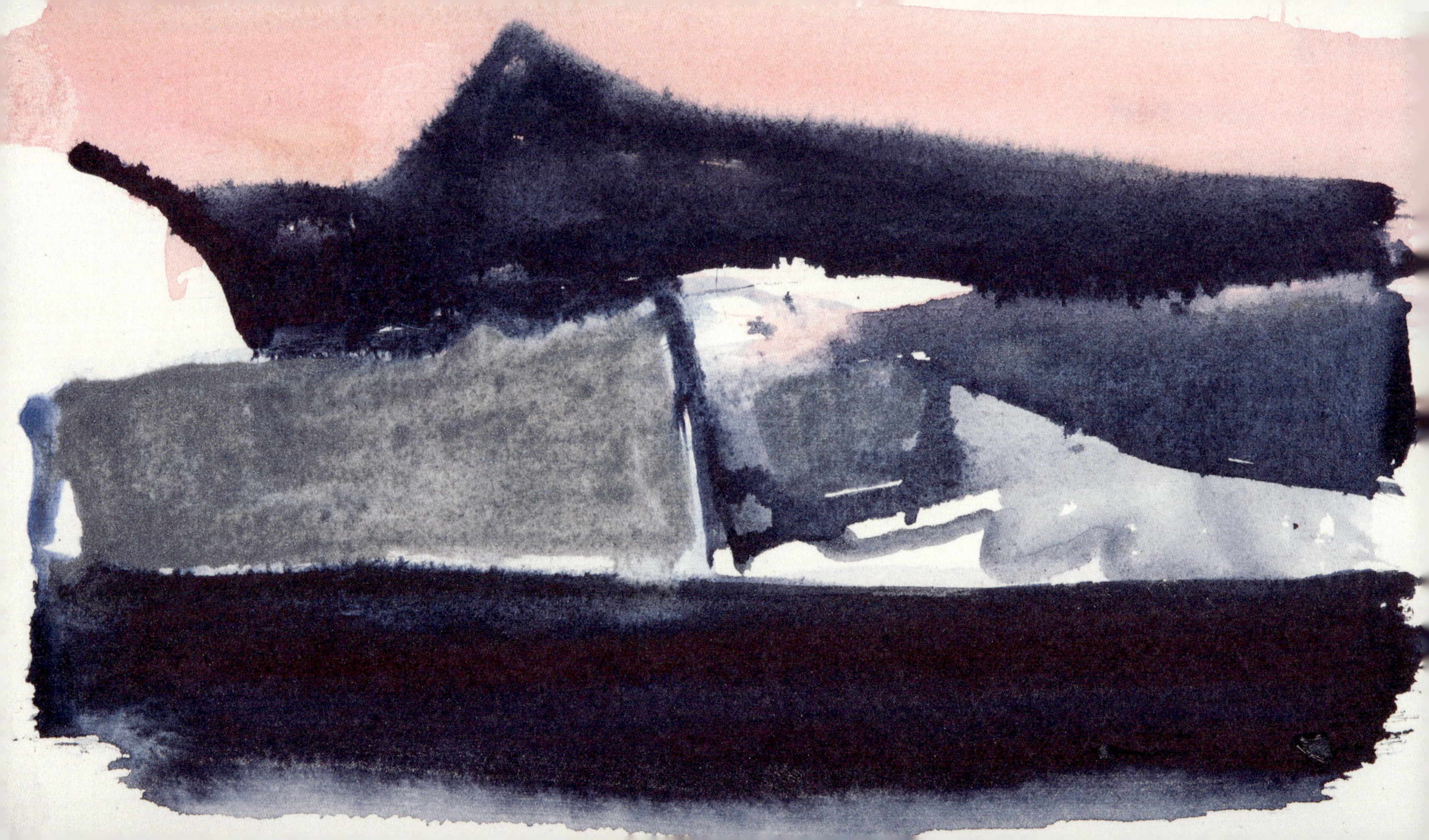

Aug 15
Sail across
Baffin bay.
Sea a bit
choppy.
A few Icebergs
Heading for Ice
to sea village
Grey skies

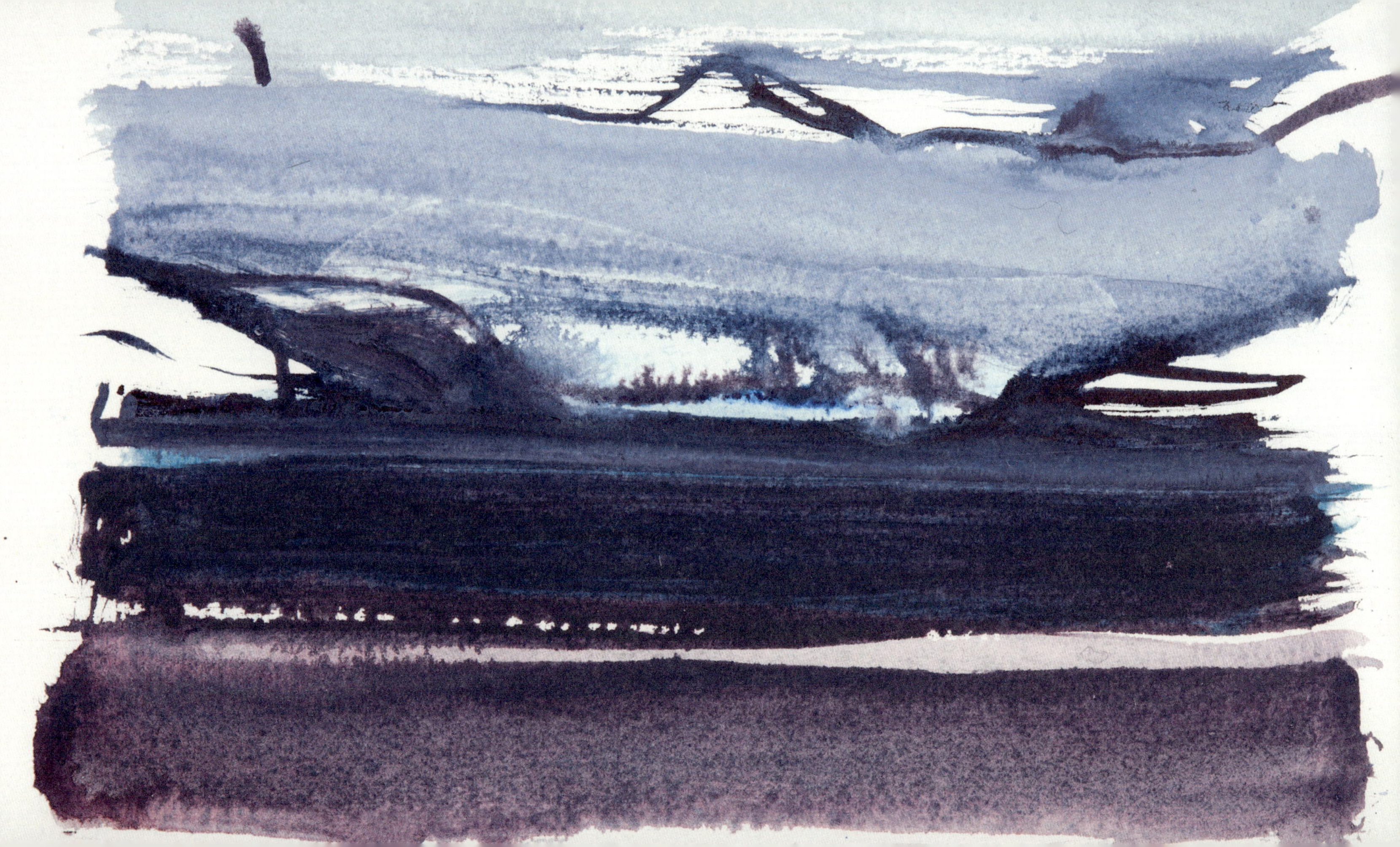

Aug 15.
Still sailing
across Baffin
Bay – Hope to
see wildlife
later..
Heading for
Pond inlet.

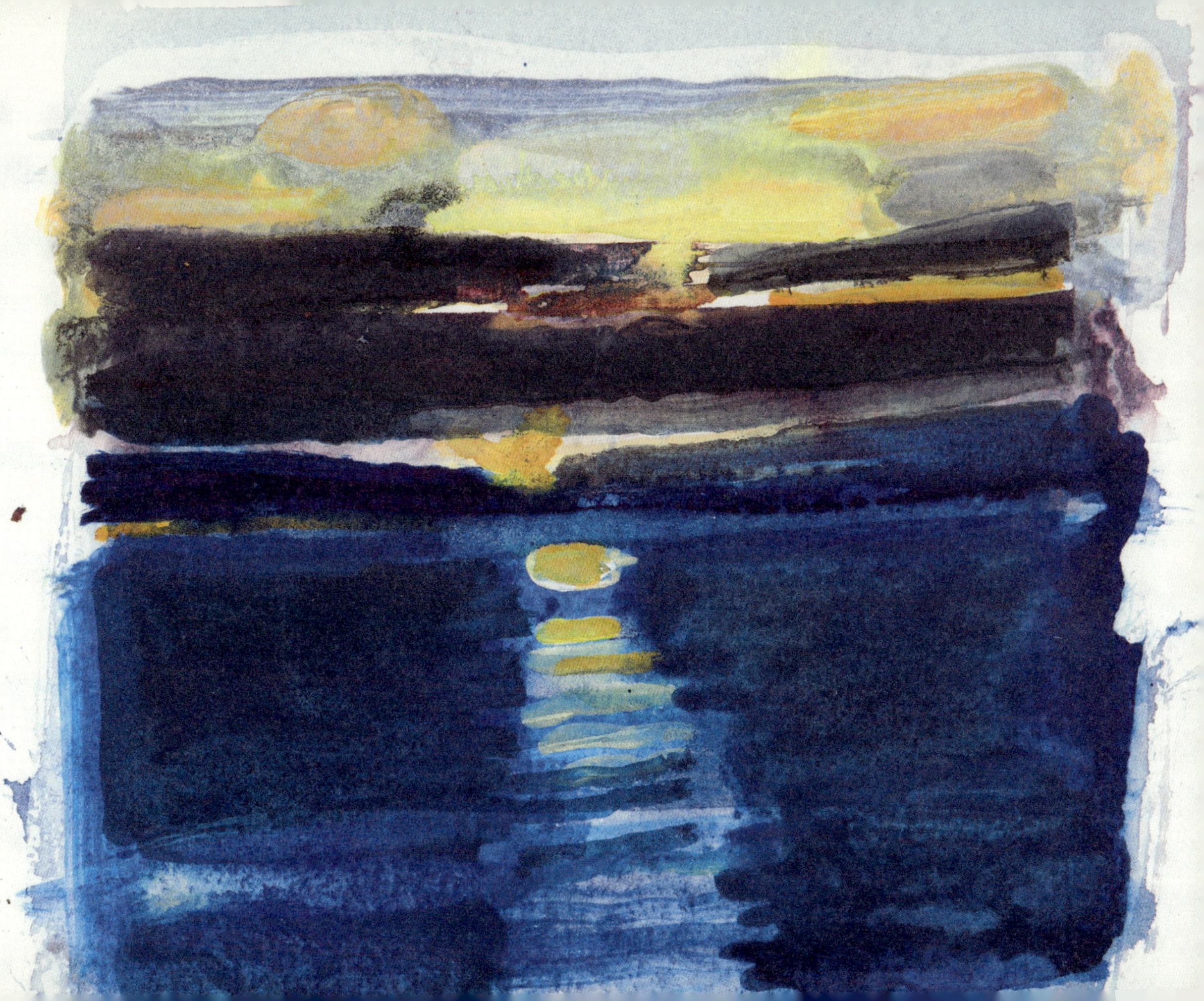

Aug 16 cont.

Pond inlet.
a sad settlement, dull and grey in comparison to the village in greenland. The Inuit put on a display of songs, local dress and Arctic games. all of which are the result of long winter nights.
crafts are poor and could do with government input to re-energise artists.

waiting here at Pond Inlet as there was a medical crisis which required our ships doctor. (luckily a trauma + emergency doctor.
The time waiting for her was taken up with an abortive attempt to land on Bylot to see the glaciers. Sea too choppy - luckily abandoned!
Beautiful sunset
Will sail overnight through Lancaster Sound.
No sign of wildlife.

Aug 16.
Arrived overnight
to Pond inlet on
Baffin Island.
Village looks over
to Bylot Island.
a still calm day
with low clouds
over the mountains
awaiting Immigration
and customs.
Looking over to
glaciers on Bylot.
Sailing over to
Bylot National
Park.

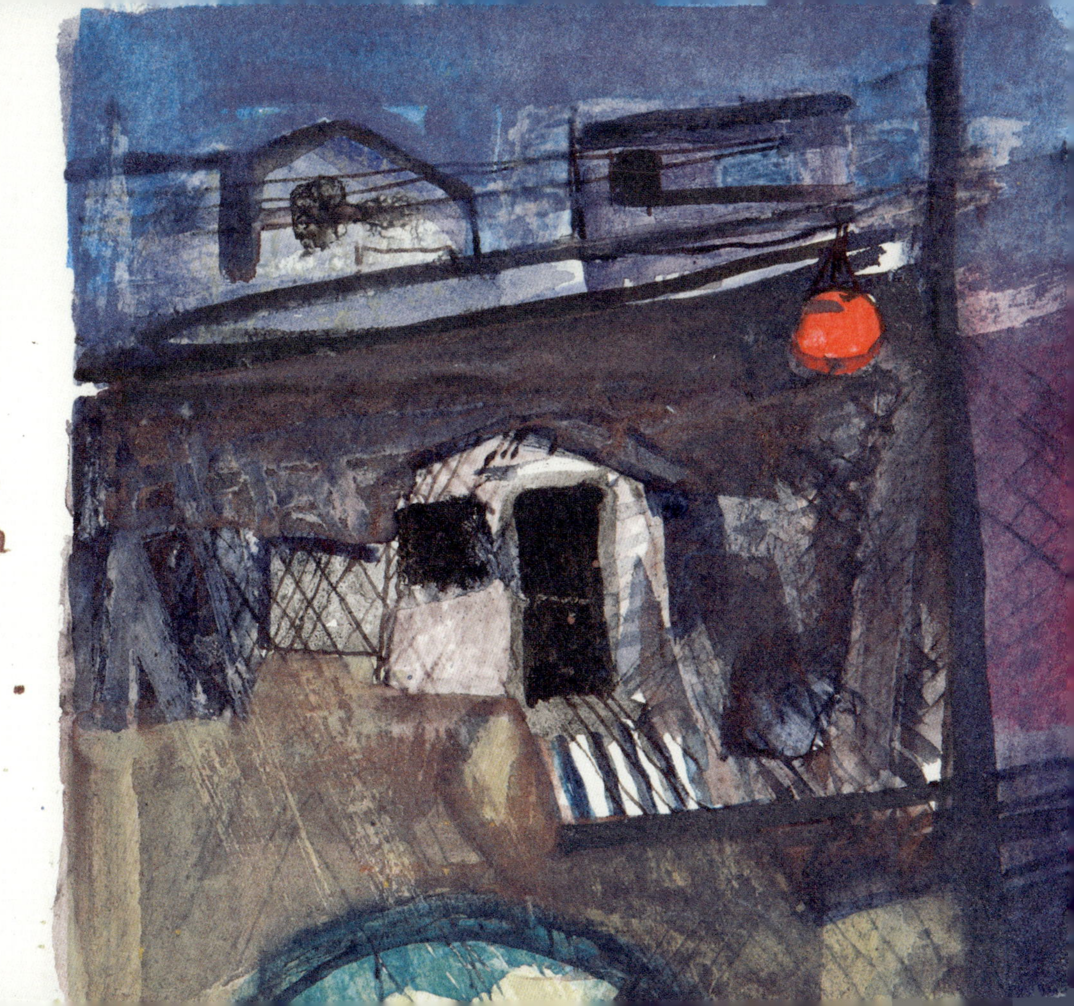

Aug 16
Nightfall crossing
Lancaster Sound

Aug 17
Sailing to Dundas
Harbour. Landing
there around 10 AM
Devon Island.
Landed on island.
Saw some archeology
sites - walrus skull
arctic mosses, mushrooms
and flowers - various
animal droppings but
no animals on land
but some seals in the
bay.

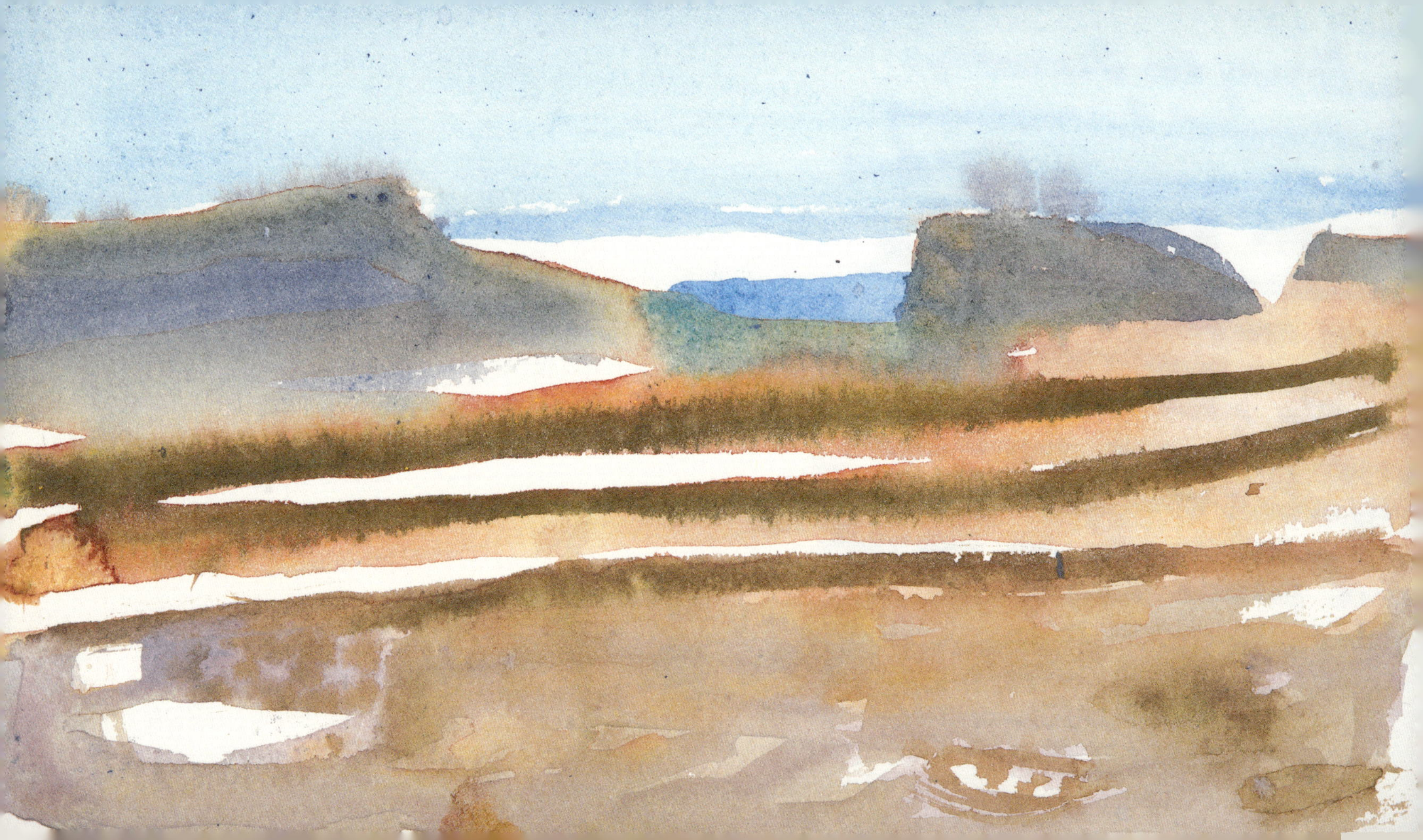

Aug 18
Sail to Beechy
Island.
Landed on Beechy
Very cold, stoney
beach with many
fossils - The graves
of three of Franklin's
men and one from
the Investigator
Saw food depot
from sea.
Radstock Bay
Caswell Tower
Landed to see
muskox and
old settlements
with many
whale bones.

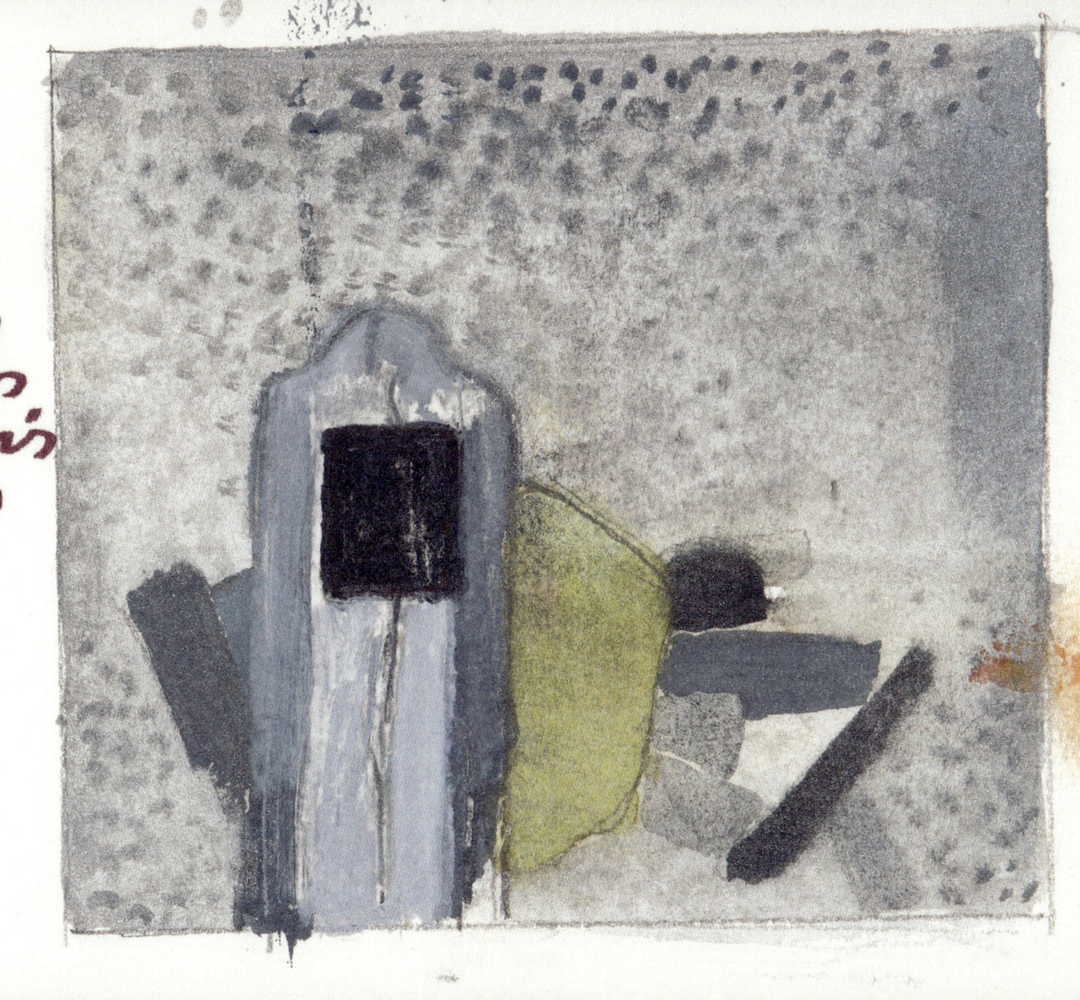

19 aug.
Prince Leopold
Island.
Bird Sanctuary
go by zodiac
to cliff face.
250 metres high
sedimentary
rock.
Not as many
birds as I
expected.
Prince Leopold
Harbour.
Port Leopold.

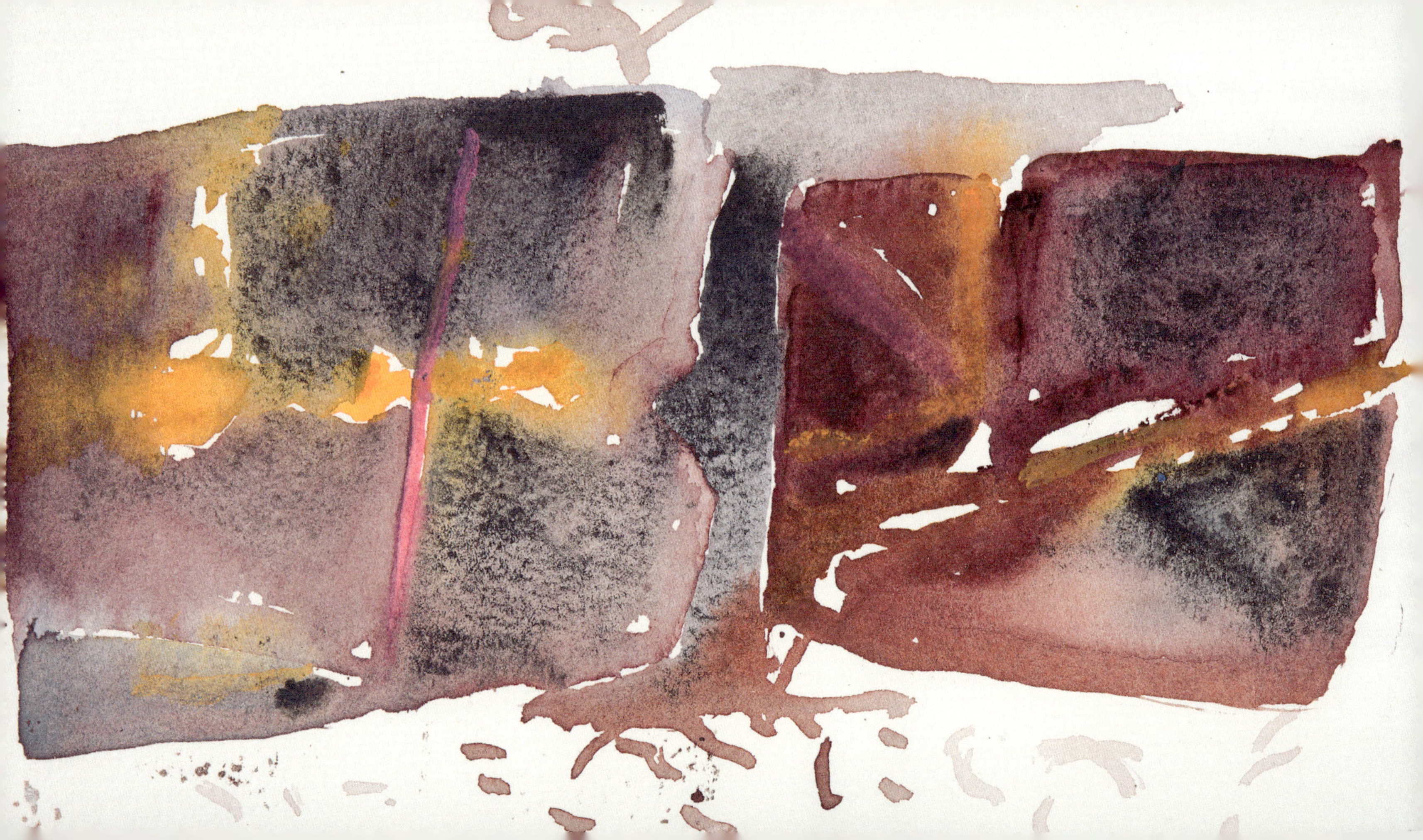

20 aug.
Prince Regent
Inlet to Fort Ross
on Somerset Island.
Cresswell Bay
Hudson's Bay Trading
Post.

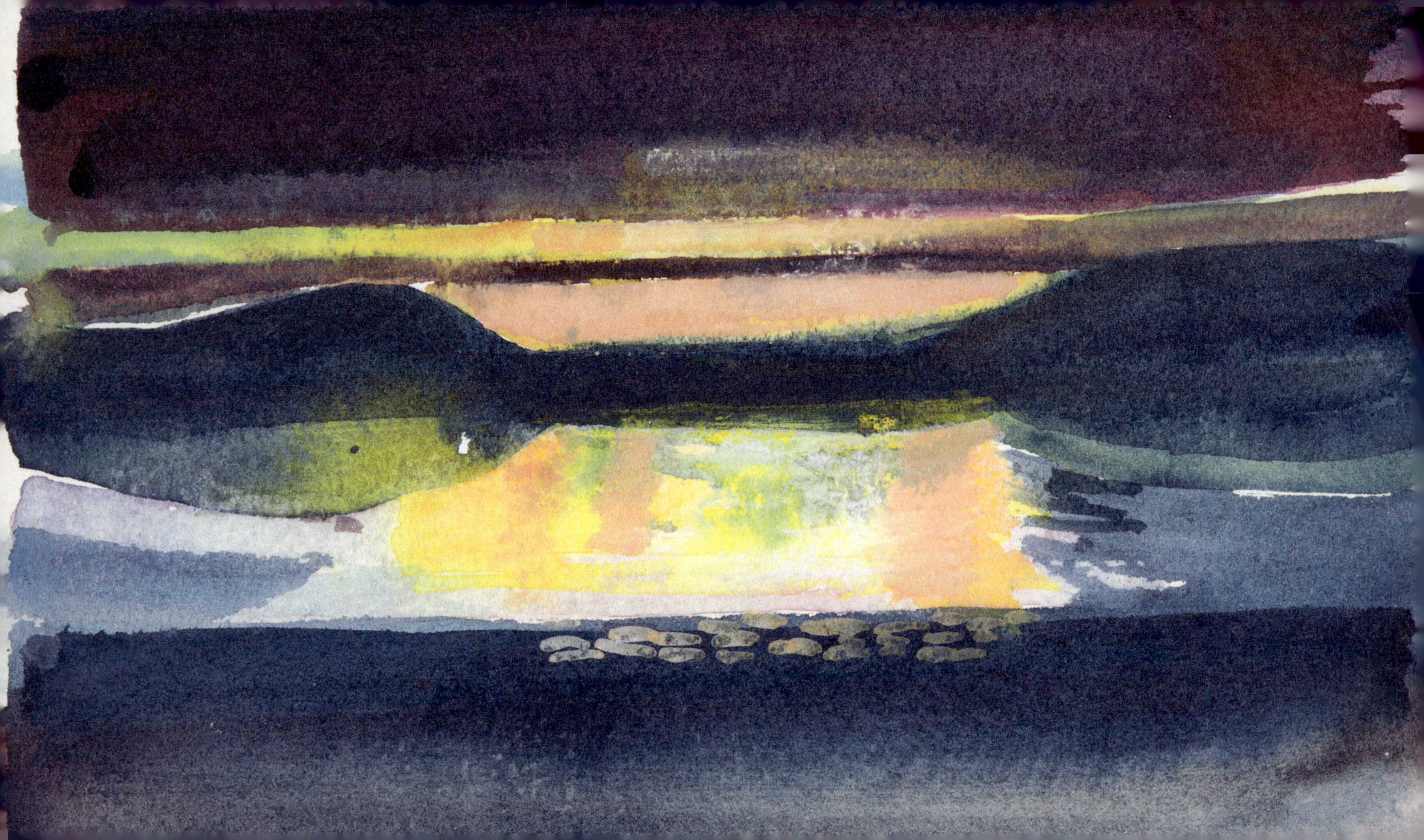

Bellot Strait
20 aug.
Sailed through
this narrow
strait in the evening
as the sun was setting
currents coming in
opposite directions from
the Pacific and the
atlantic:
at one point the
passage is 0.5 k wide
emerging into the
Peel Sound and
Franklin Strait.

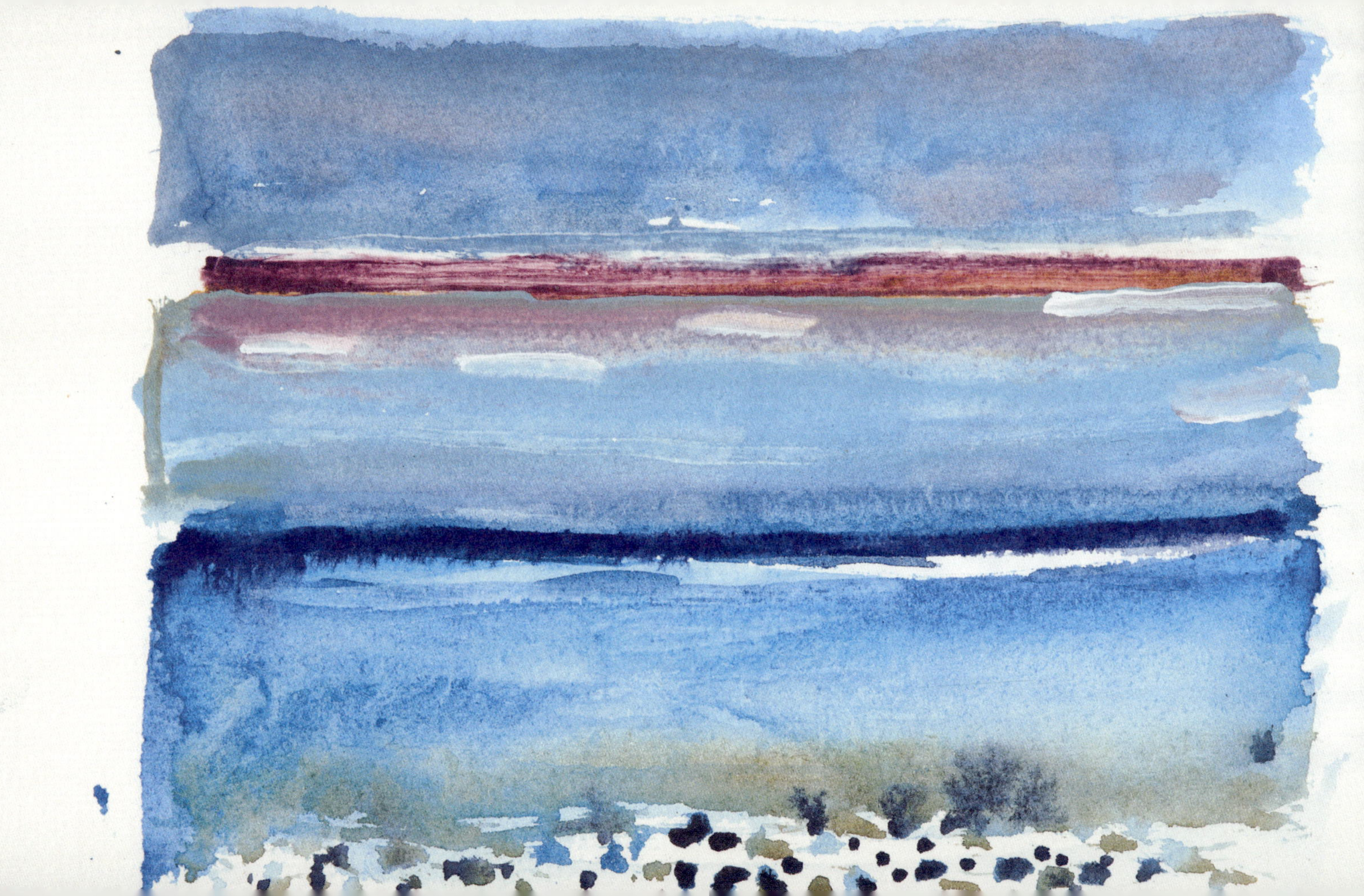

21 aug
Prince of Wales
Island
Franklin Strait
Conningham Bay
5 Polar bears
eating Beluga
whales.

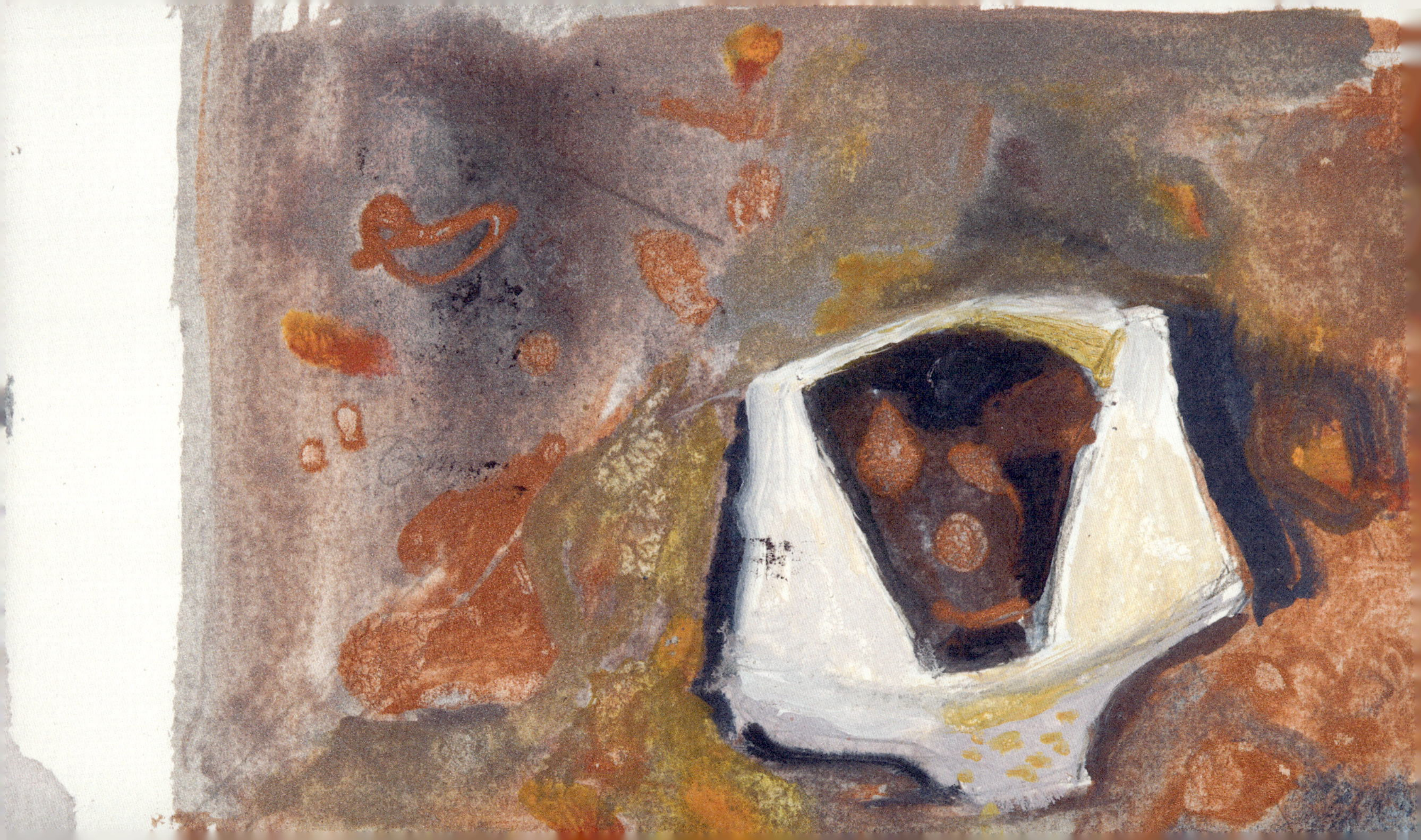

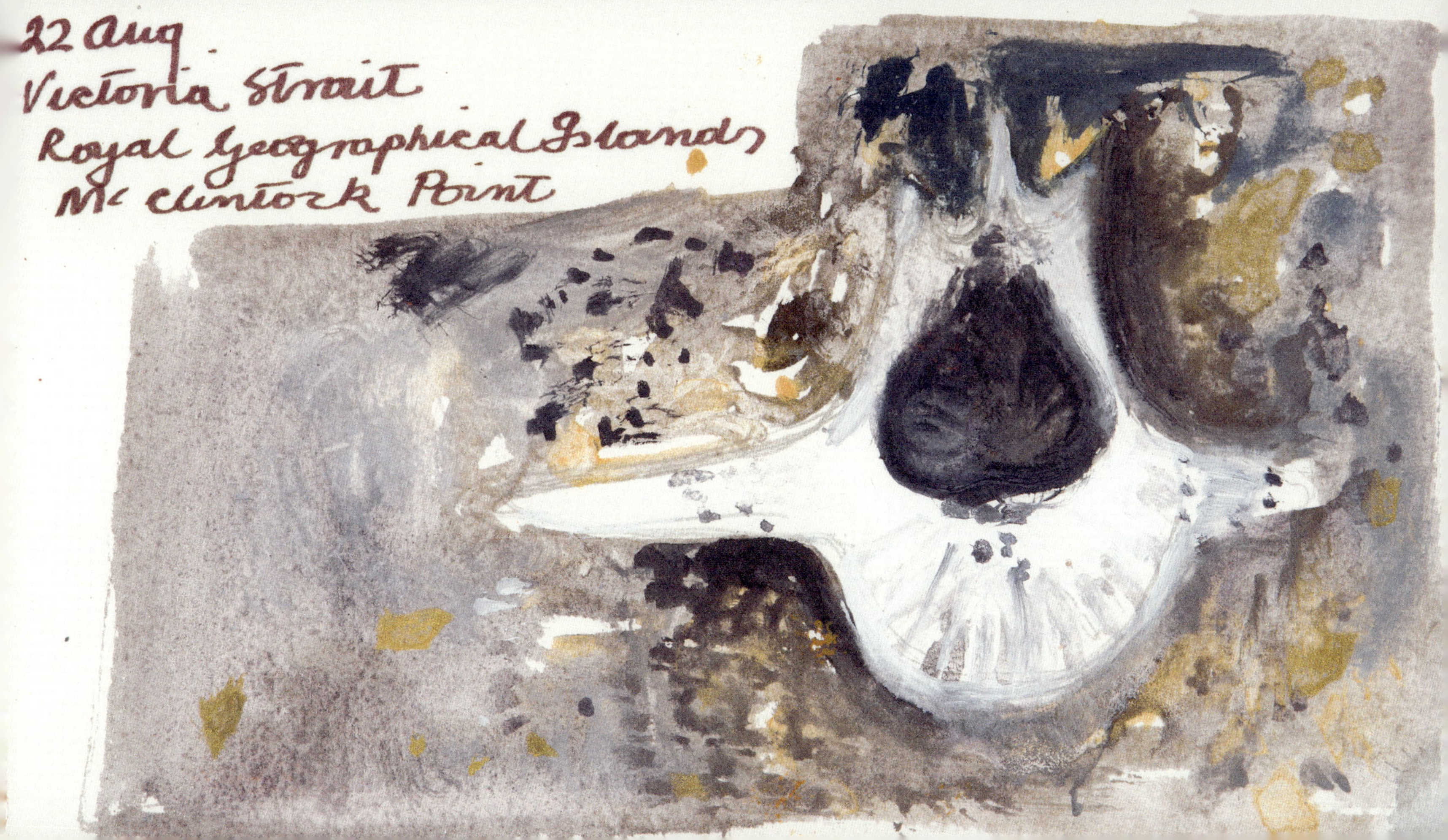
22 Aug.
Victoria Strait
Royal Geographical Islands
Mc Clintock Point

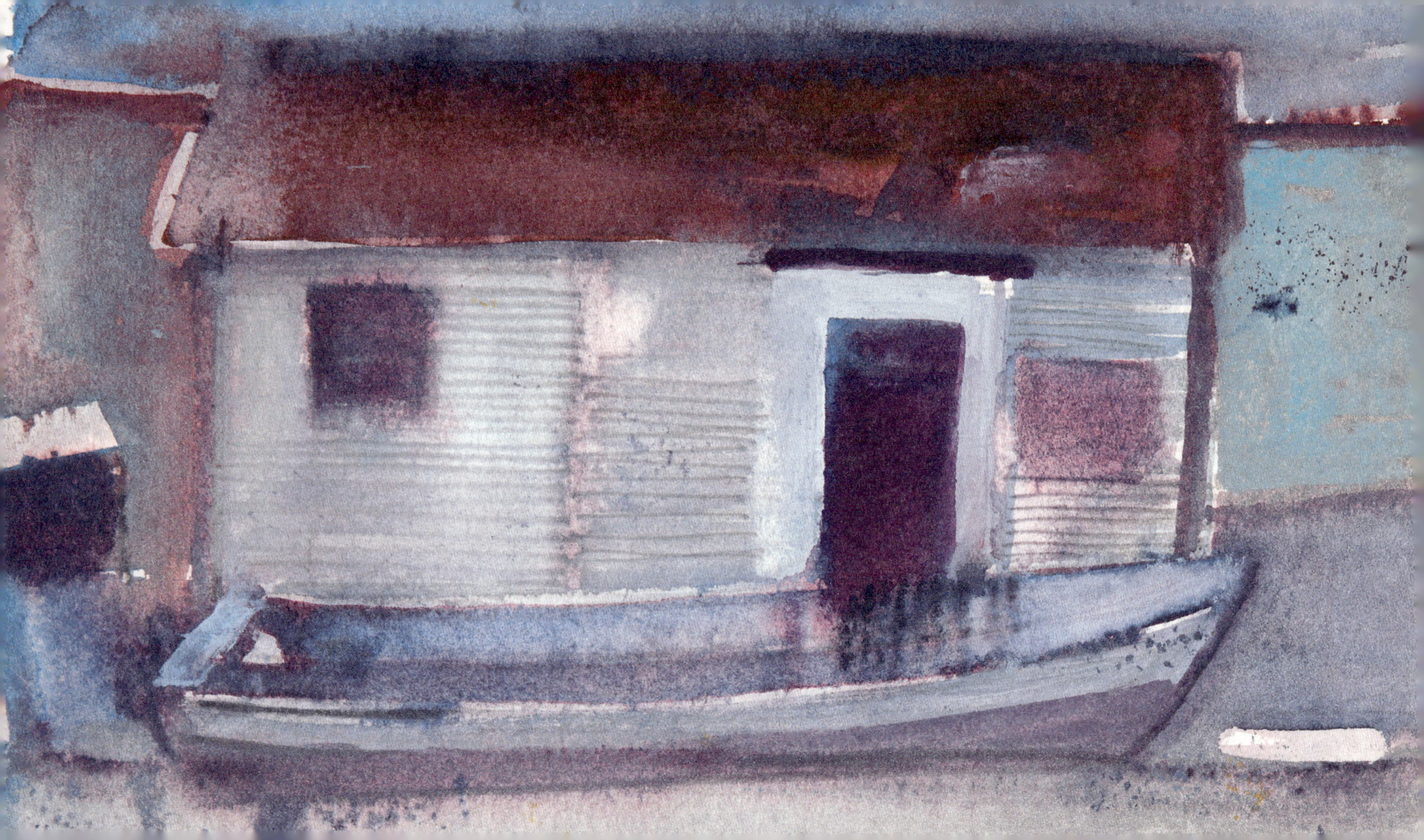

3 aug. -
Cambridge Bay
Morning -
Big settlement
Sunday
morning
Waited at airport
for 3 hours as no
fuel for plane.
Had to wake up
tanker driver.
Flight to Edmonton
Bus to Fairmont
Said goodbye to
friends.

North West Passage 2016
Barbara Davis Rae

Flight to Kangerlussuaq from Copenhagen
Stayed at airport hotel. Good beds and shower
but no lift for luggage. Had a day long
trip to Russell glacier and the ice cap.
Really spectacular. On the following day
we took a flight by twin prop plane
down Paradise Valley then out over the
glacier and ice cap. Amazing!
We saw the airport museum dedicated
to the USA airbase established here in
the cold war period of the 50's.
First night we had a meal in the Boat
Club. (Generous portion of prawns) then the
next night had a superb dinner in the
airport restaurant – liquorish creme brullee!!

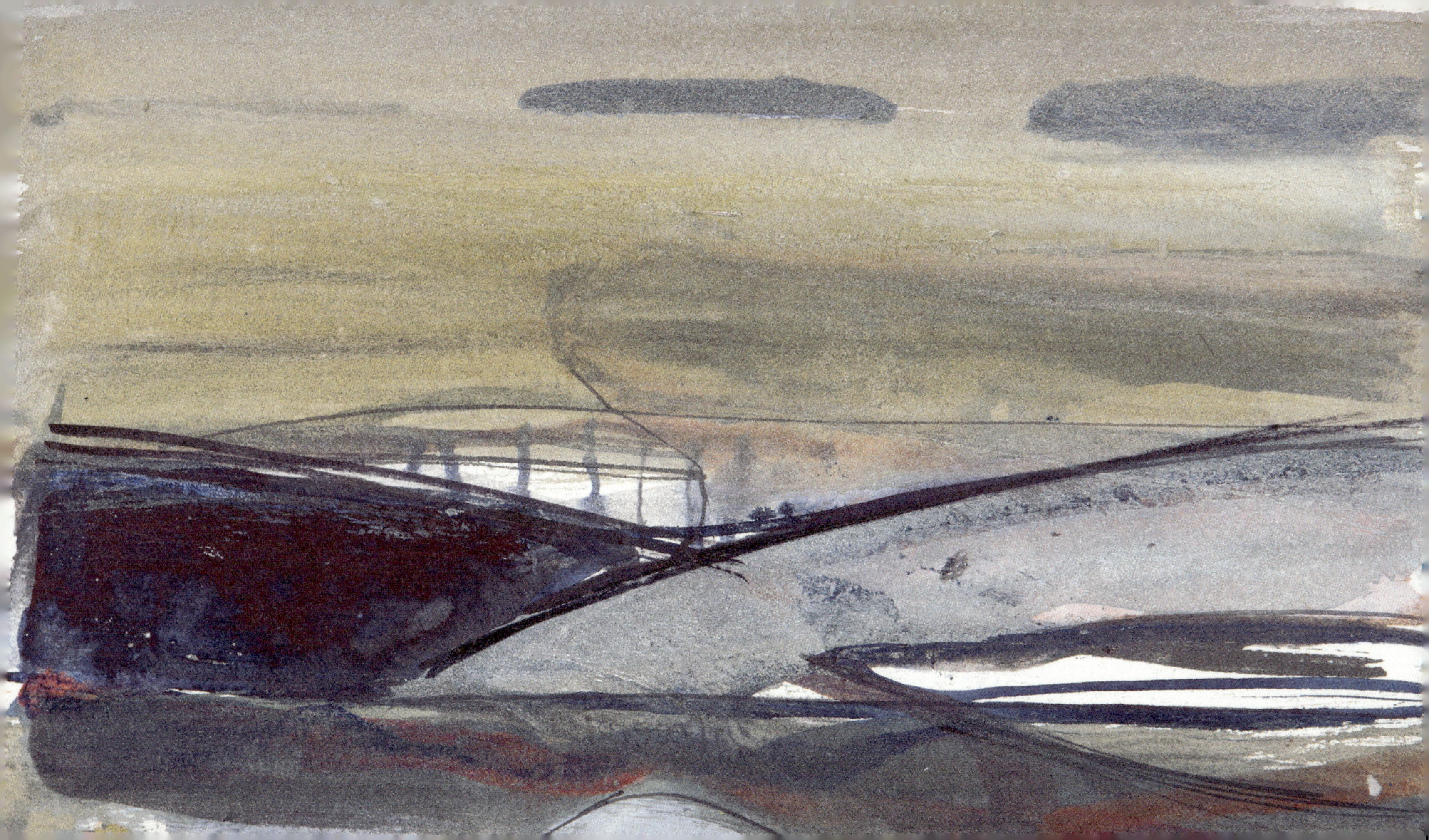

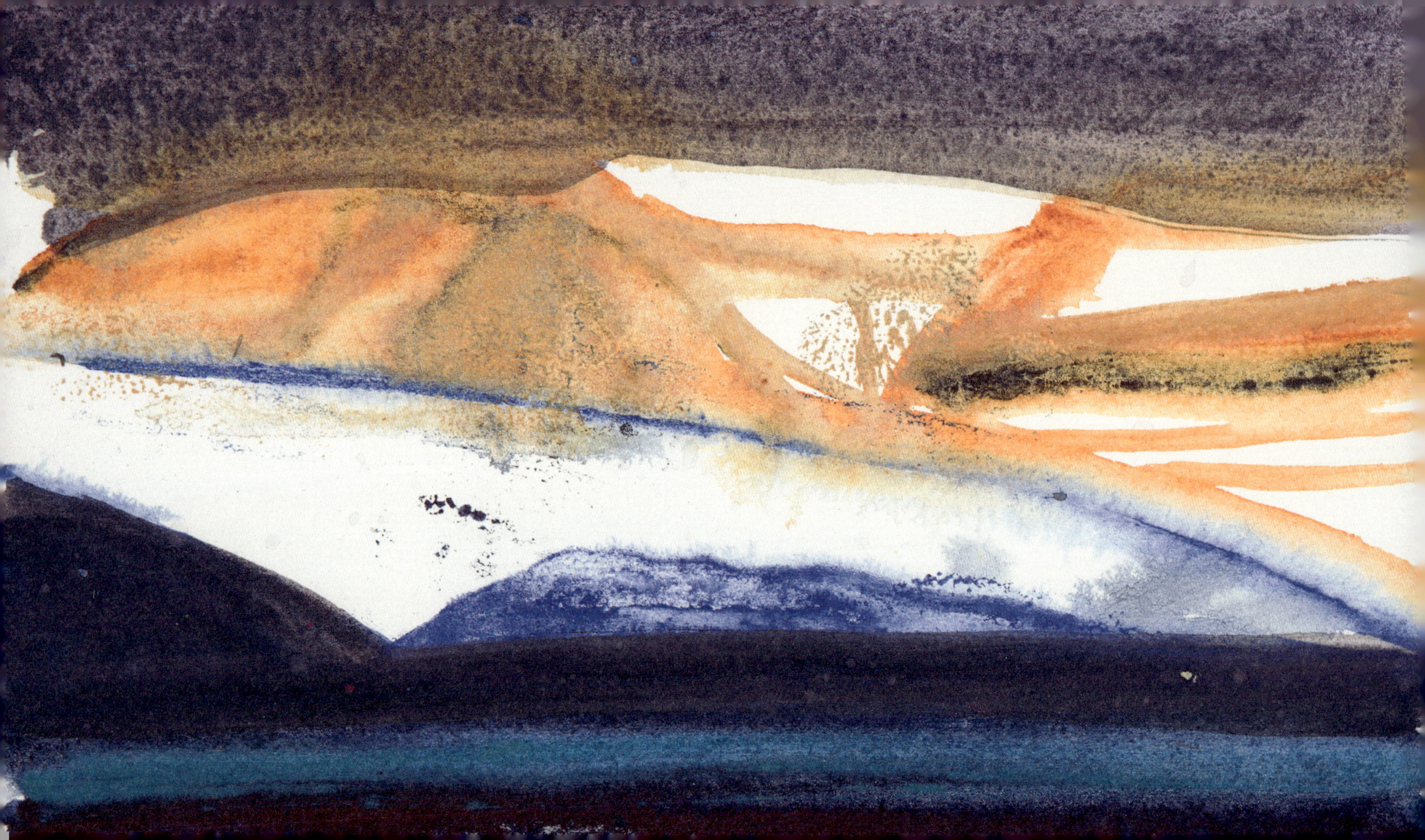

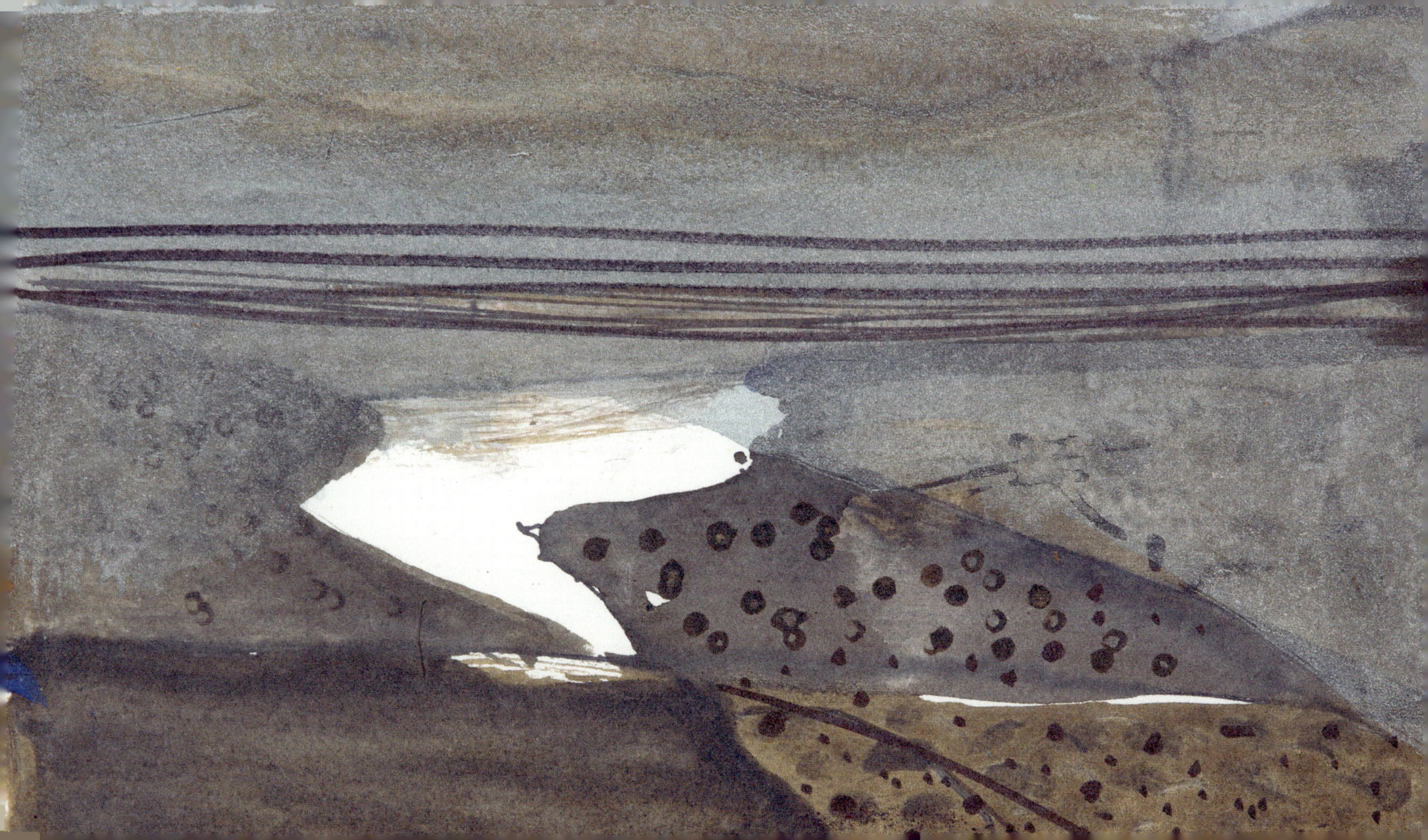

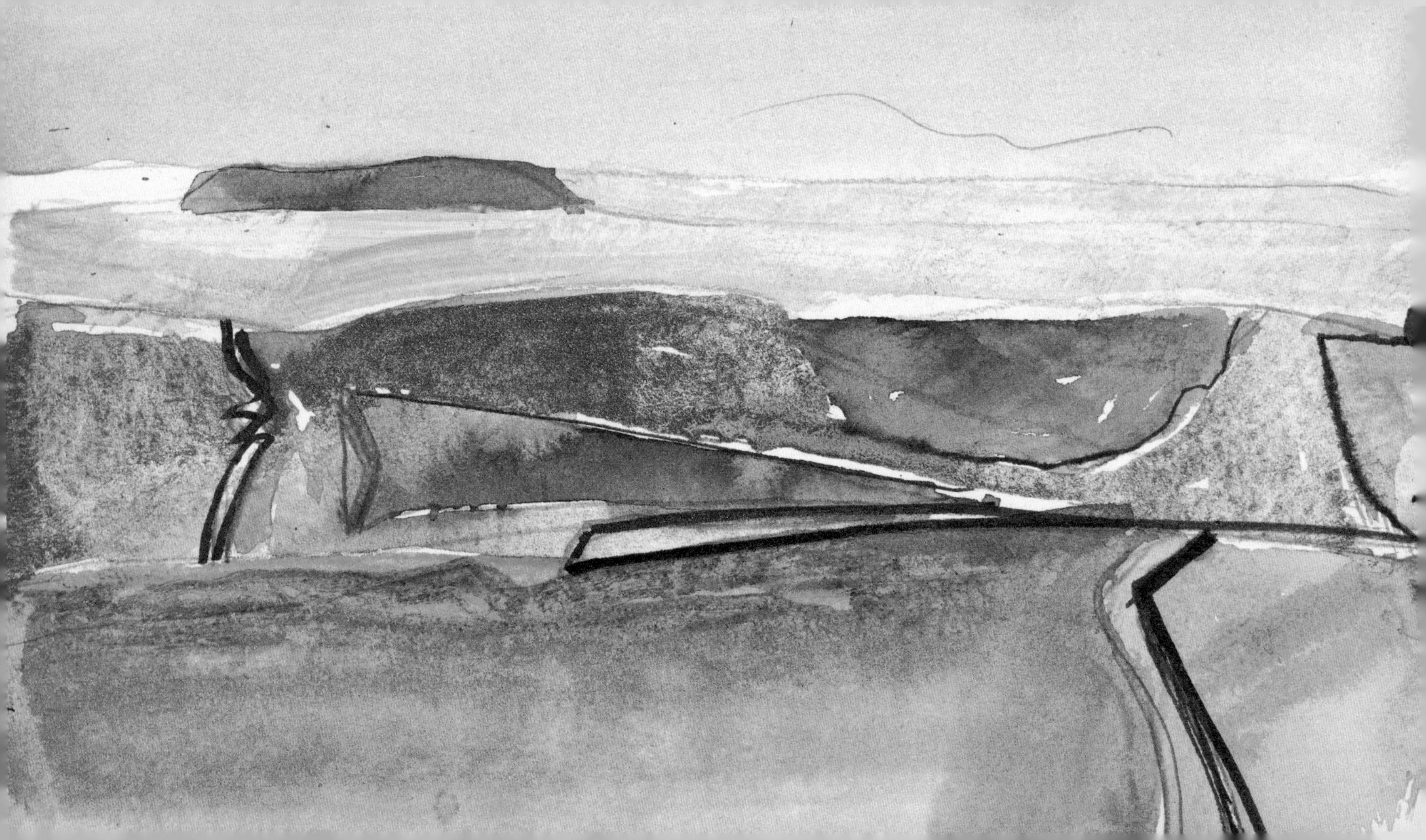

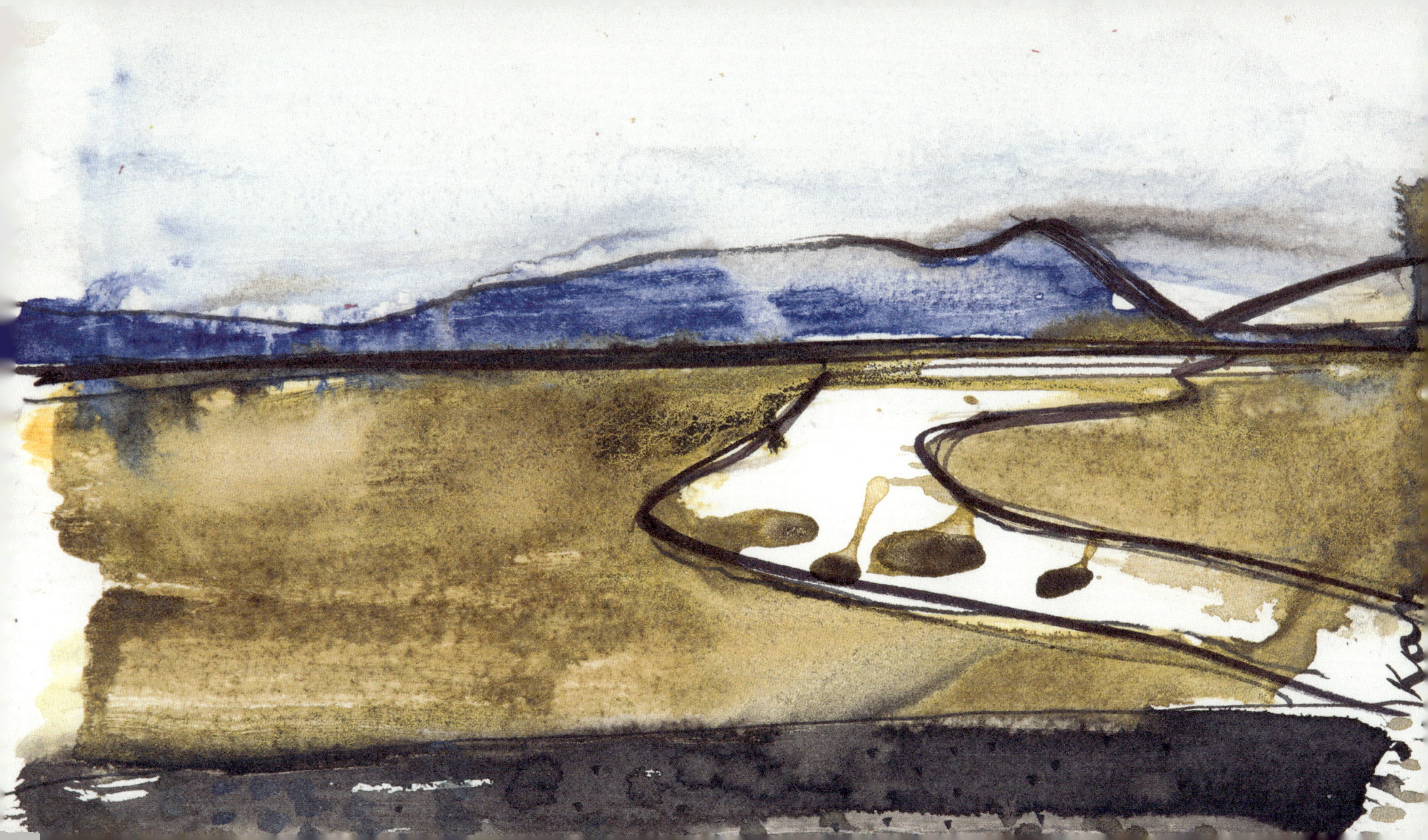

Boarded the boat after taking a Taxi along to the pier to look at the historic graffiti on the rocks above the harbour where the Vavilov was moored.

We conquered with the film maker in tow. The next day was incredibly warm so we wandered round Sisimiut. We had a splendid picnic at a table beside a shop selling musk ox products. Wonderfully soft and warm wool. Visited all the historic buildings on the museum site. The church on the hill was beautiful with subtle construction details. Did the wood come from Denmark?

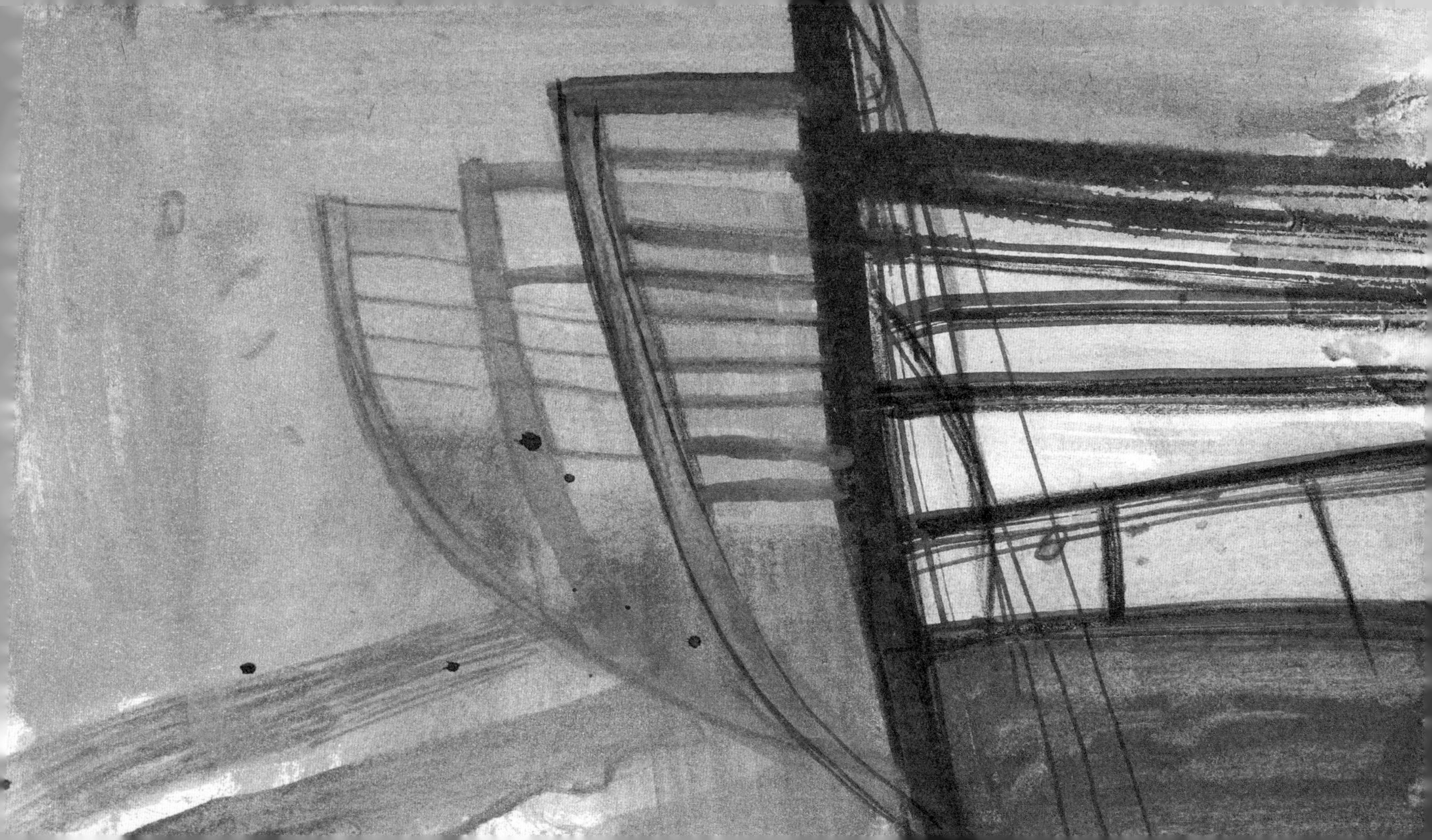

Old Hut near Sissimut Museum
a wonderful sunny day

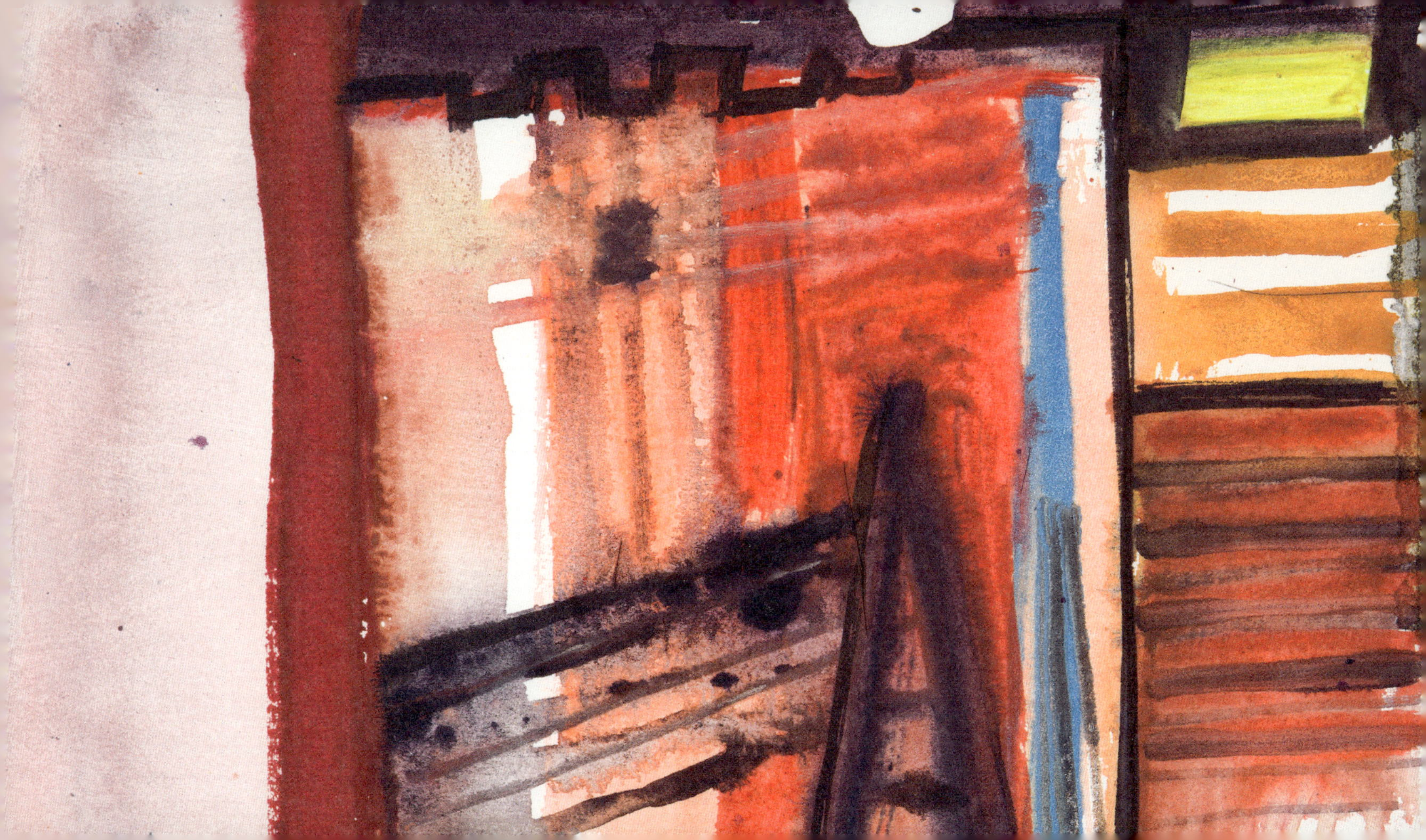

Arrived at ice free, Ilulisat harbour. Zodiac trip round the icebergs at the mouth of the glacier. Stunning warm sunshine revealing these monumental shapes. Black shadows and crystal like ice bergs.

The afternoon should have been spent either going to the museum or art gallery. Unfortunately we arrived at 3.55 to find that on a Sunday every thing closes at 4 pm.

The very busy harbour made up for that disappointment. Now sailing across Baffin Bay. Very grey day, rolling ship:

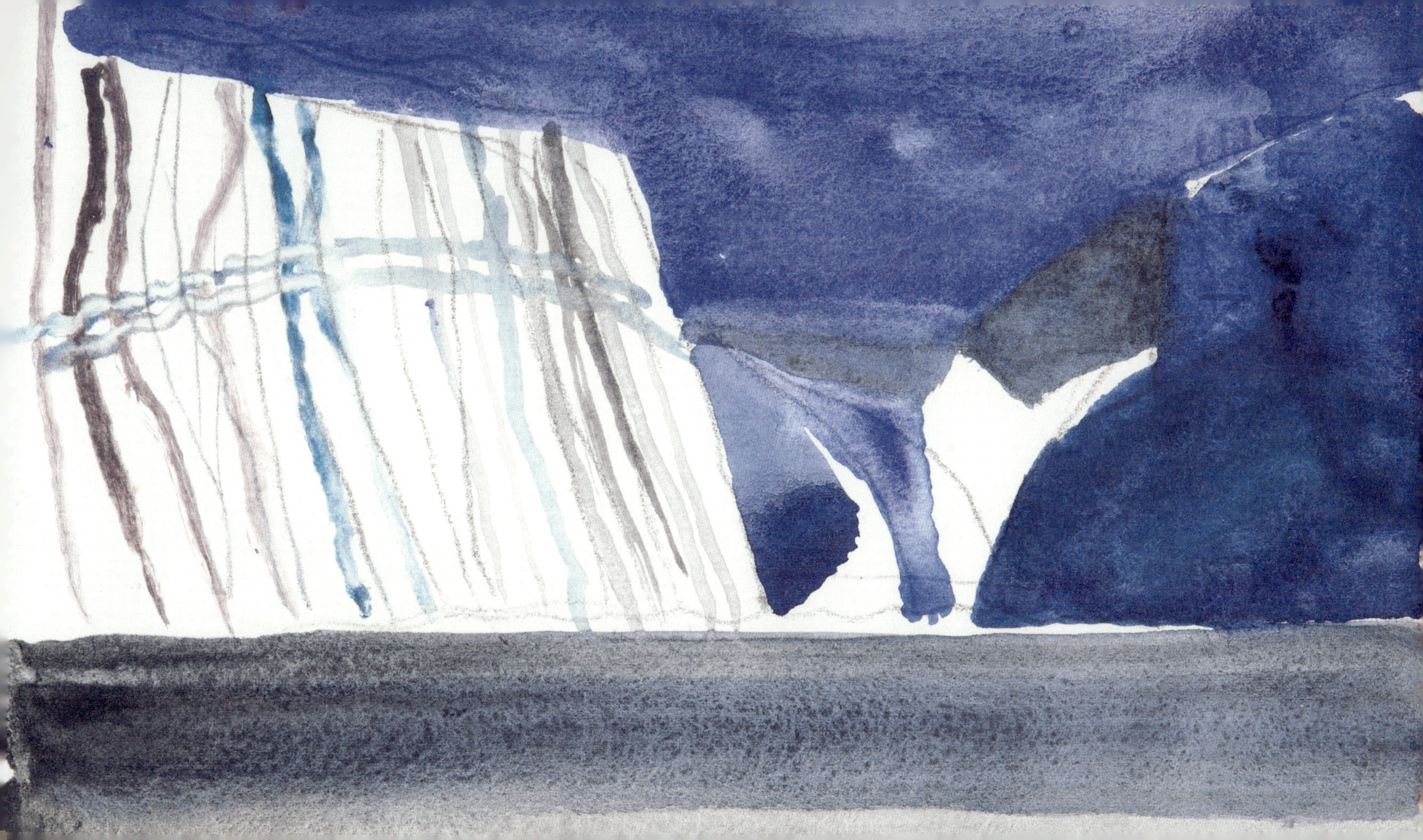

2 day sail across the bleak Baffin Bay
some whales would liven things up!
Turned my small studio/bedroom
cabin into a painting area.
The sea is rough so I am planning to
work in my cabin all day.
All shapes of individual icebergs floating
by. I am hoping to see more icebergs!

Destination now Pond Inlet.

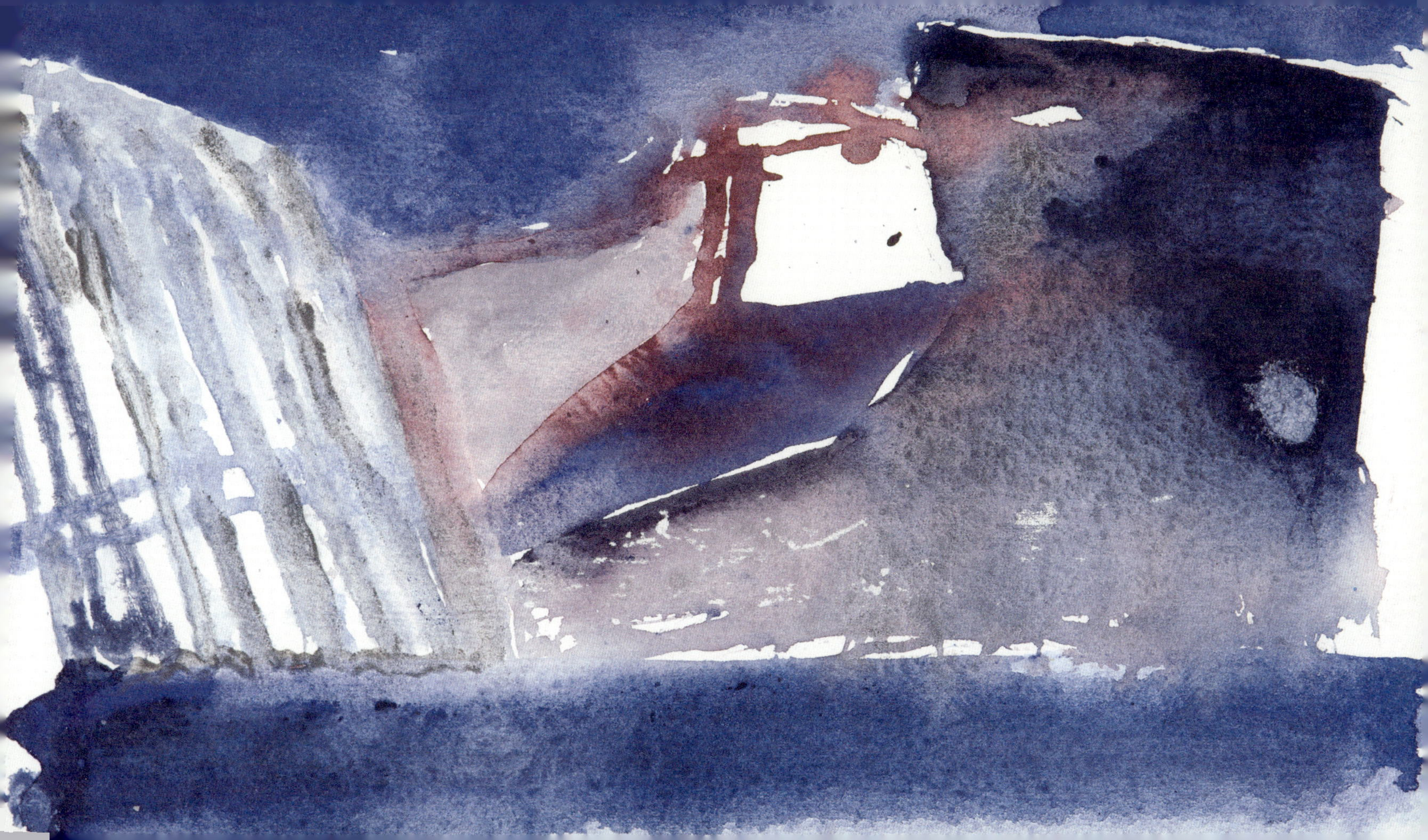

Late arrival at Pond Inlet, then held up by customs clearance.
Sat on the beach while most people went to see the cultural show at the community centre.
Today it is overcast and foggy. We are now headed to Devon Island and Dundas Harbour where there are the old RCMP huts
No landing at Dundas. Two polar bears on land. Very cold day so stayed on board to work
A few small ice bergs in the bay.

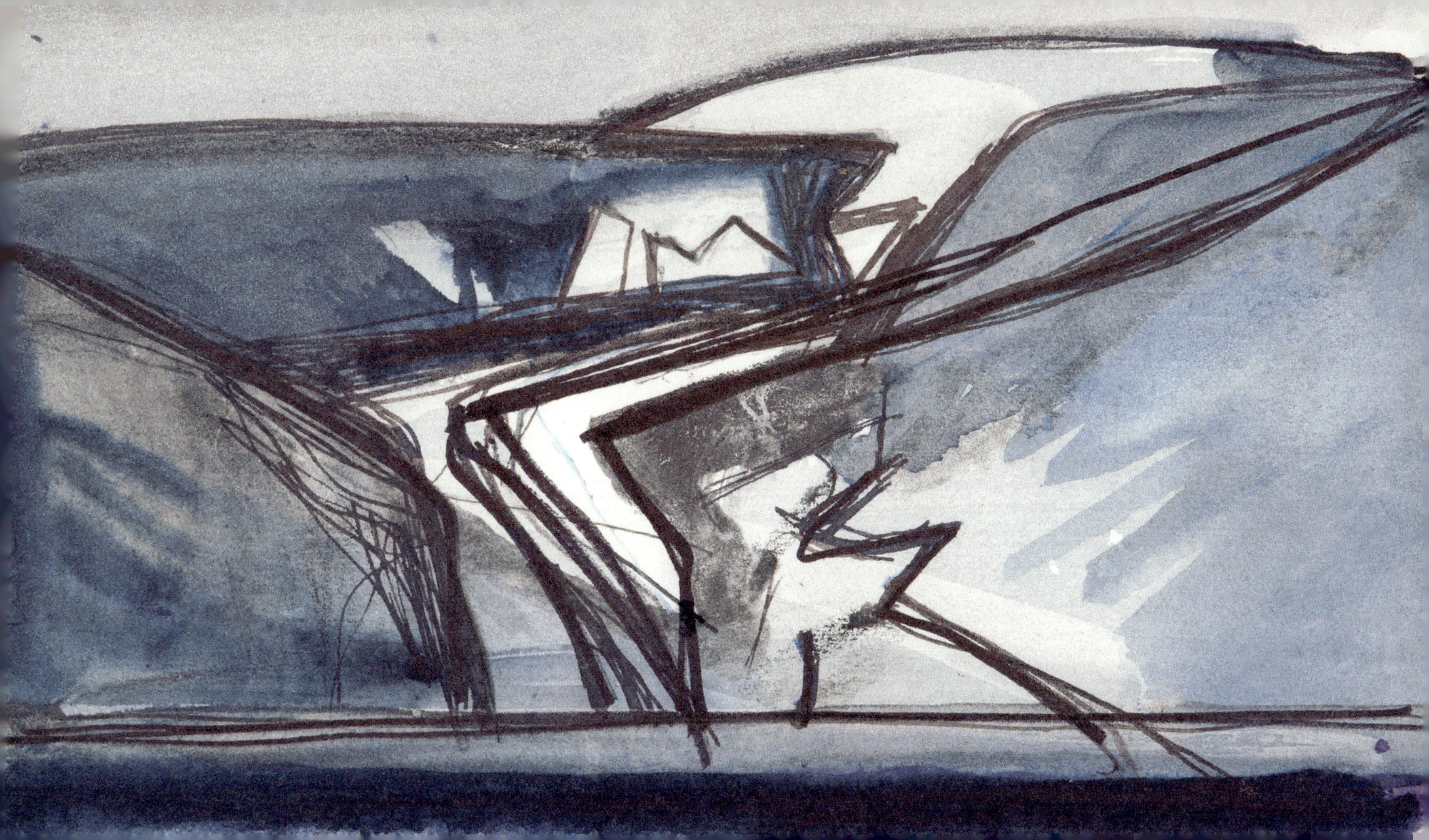

Sailed to Powell Inlet but no landing as it was too rough.
Passed by sister ship IOFFE on her way east.
Heading for Maxwell Bay. Dramatic glacier on the way.
Sailing along Deron Island – grey skies and rough seas

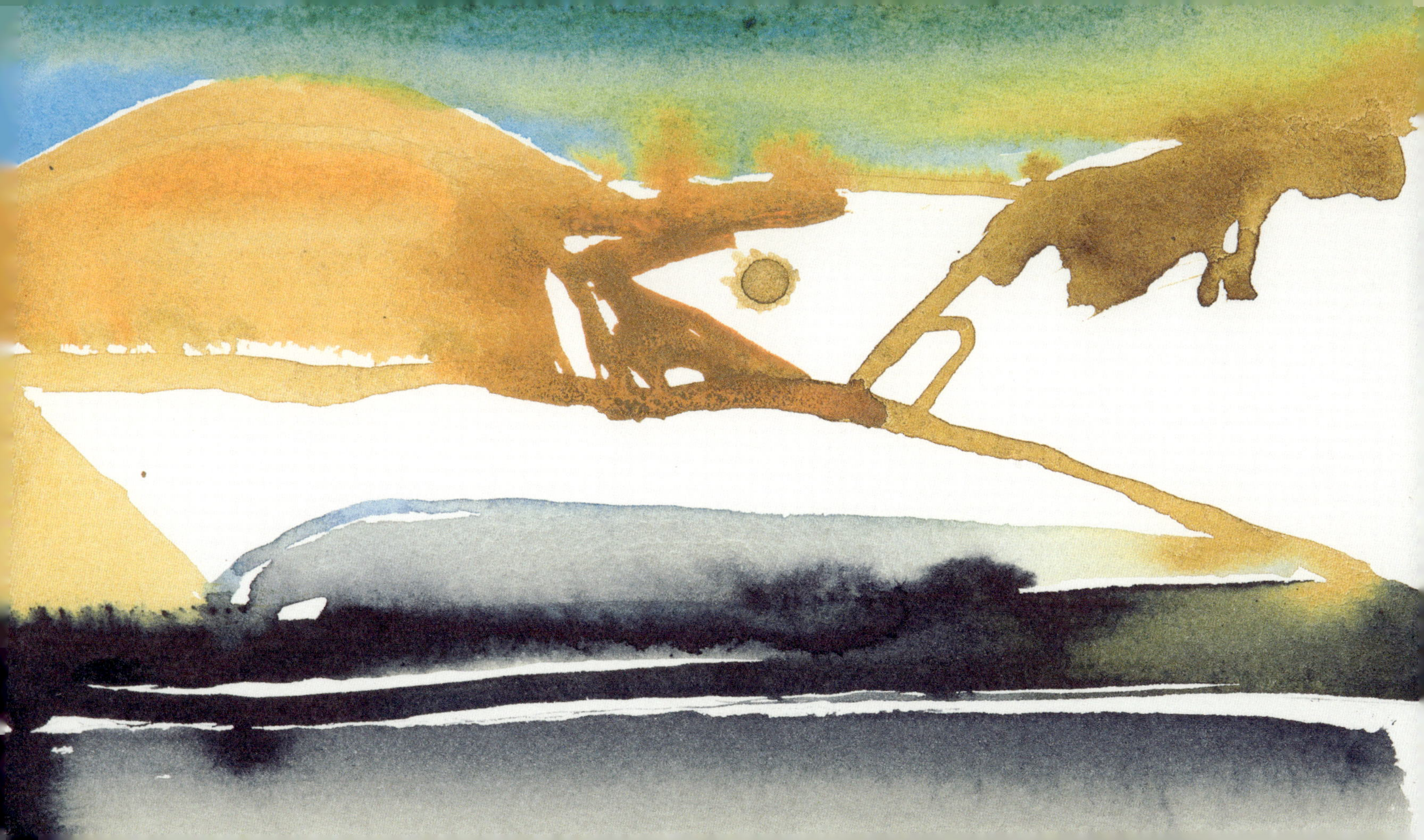

Arrived early at Beechy Island where the graves from the Franklin expedition are. A desolute bay with a raised beach of grey pebbles.. a light dusting of snow. Very windswep Further along the bay, is Northumberland hut, or the remains of it. Many rusting barrel hoops and pieces of timber from a boat or from the disintegrating hut. Rusty food cans were formed into a cross a beautiful schooner was moored in the bay.

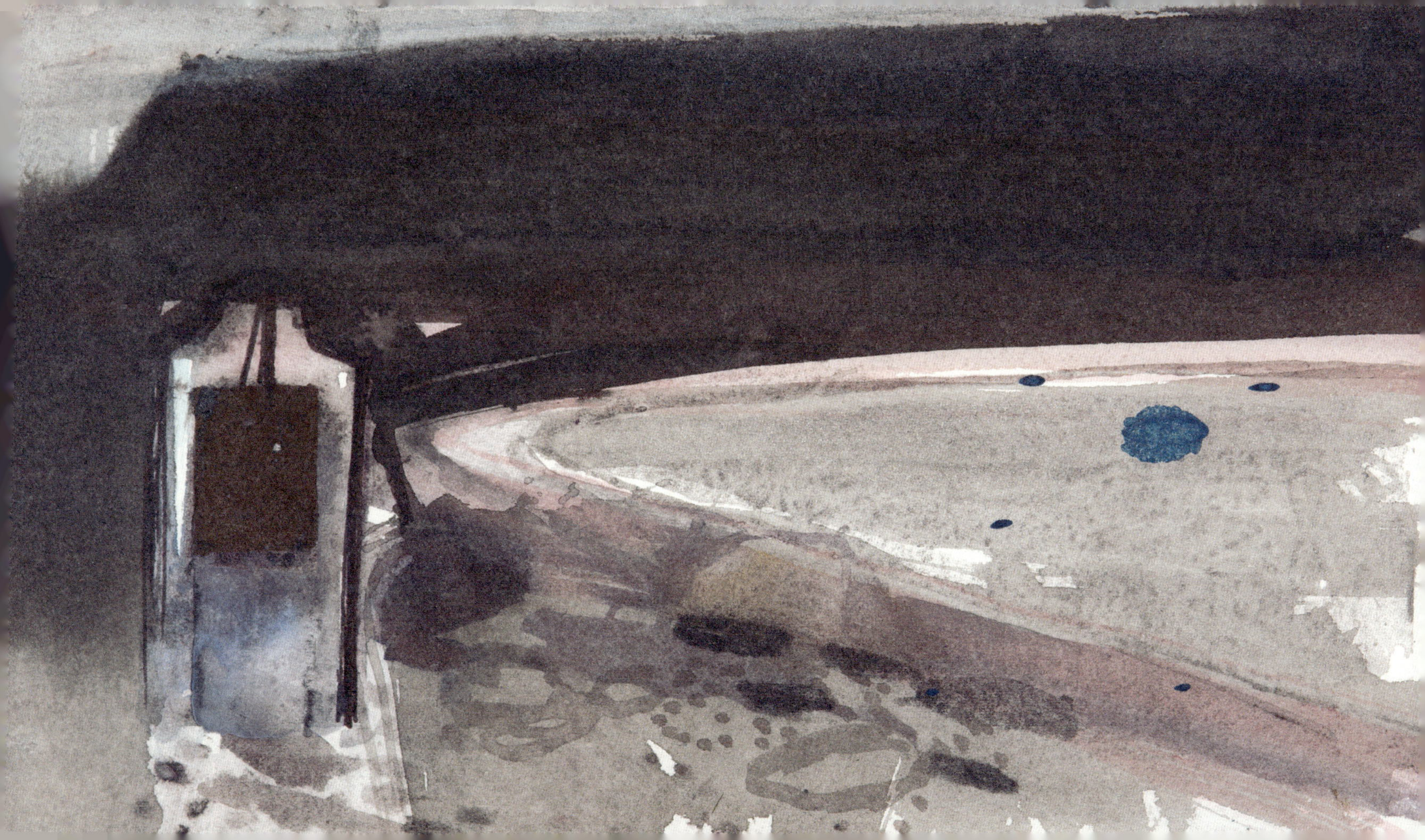

Northumberland Hut Ruins

Gradually disintegrating, more so from last year. Many people now treading the fragile tundra and taking souvenirs.

Unregulated private yaughts and the 1000 passenger Crystal Serenity is not good news for the Arctic

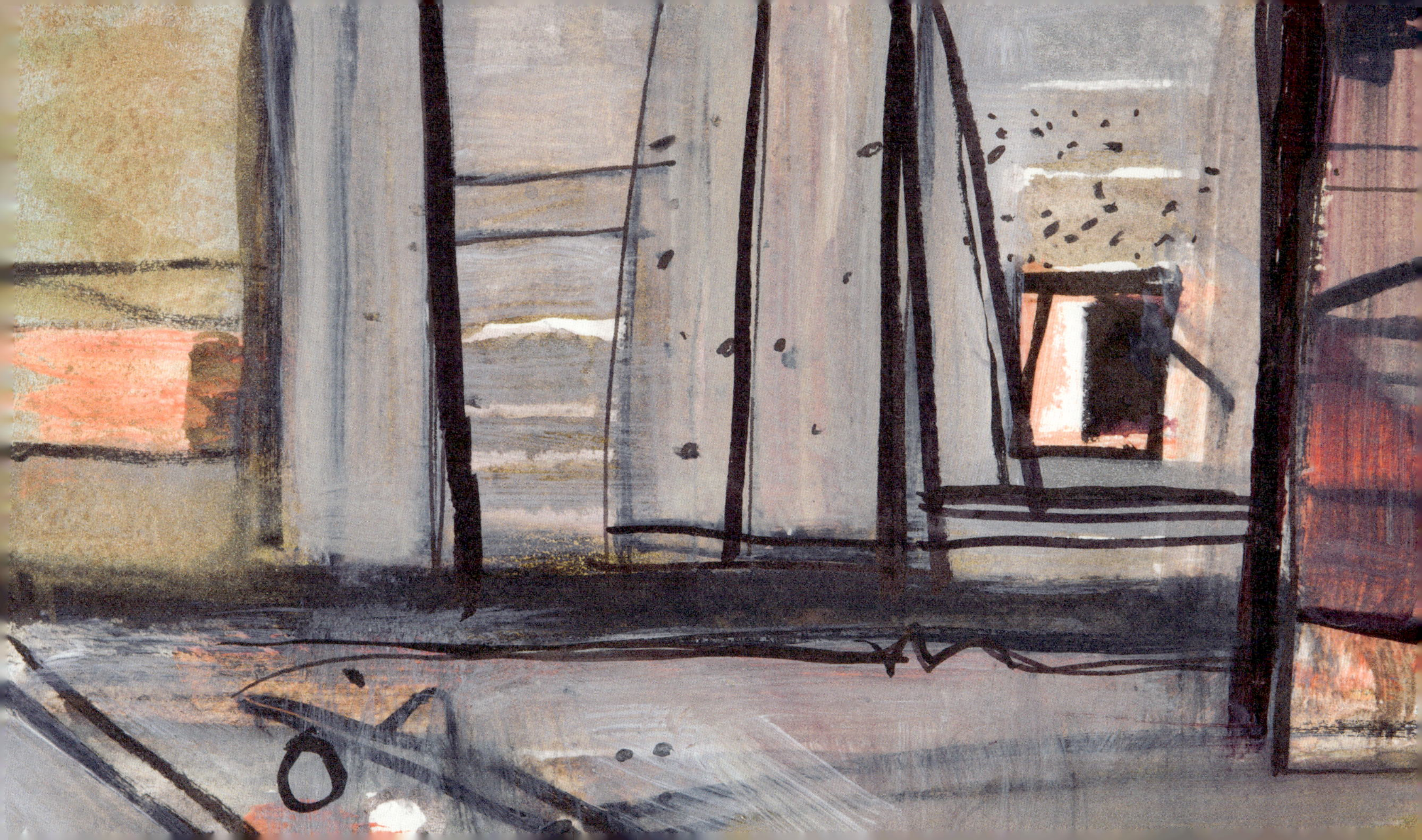

Went on to Prince Port Leopold Island
300 Metre cliffs shrouded in wispy mist.
Cruised in the zodiacs for 3 hours
Looking at the seabirds nesting there
and them flying around the boat.
Not as many as I would have
expected. Pretty cold and wet after
rain and spray for 3 Hours.
The cliffs however were spectacular.

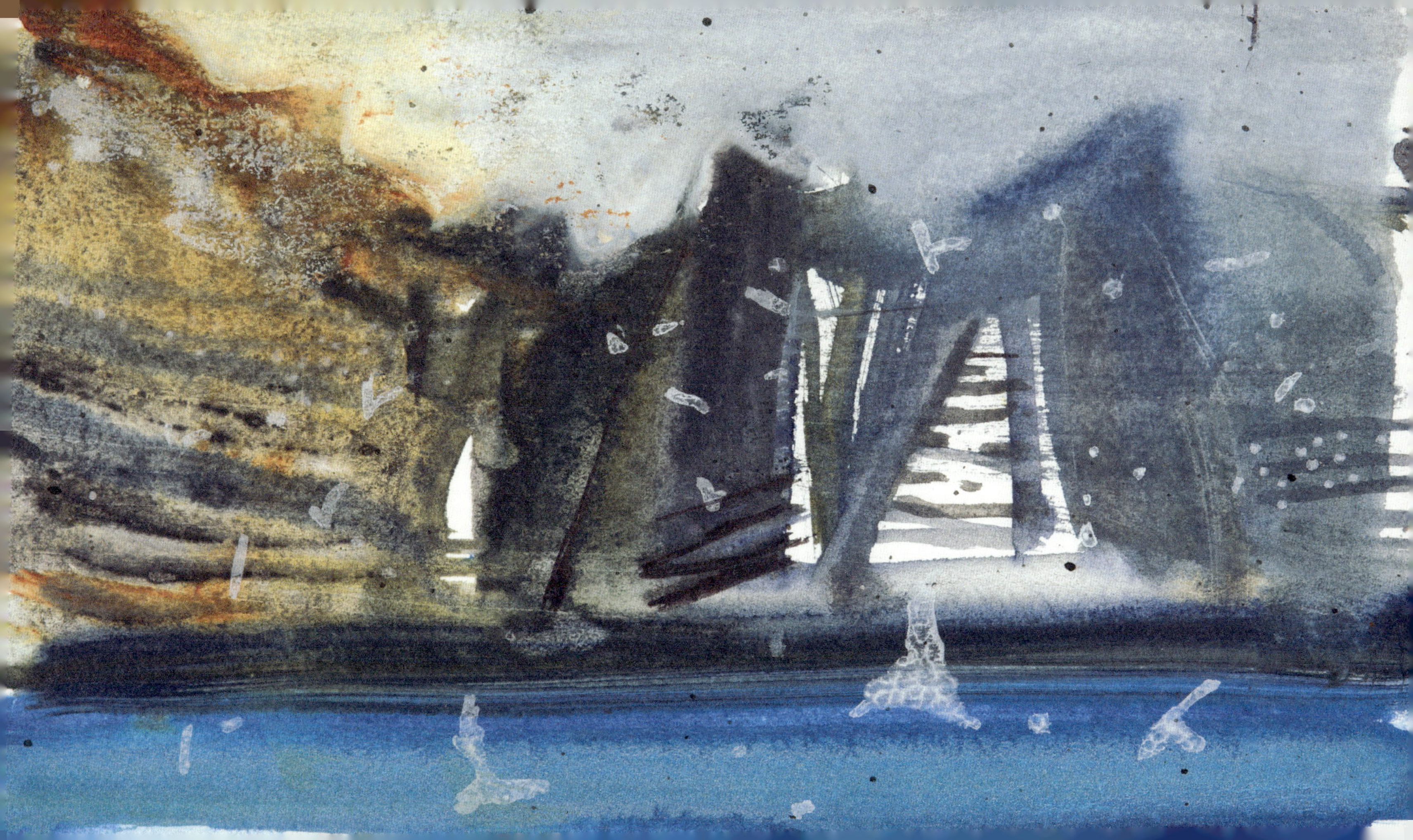

This afternoon to Port Leopold
The day was very grey, with low mist
Landed at the site of the hut. Weathered
wood, with bones, moss and old stoves
around, strewn, making a pattern in the
earth. A barren desolate place supposedly
a HBC outpost. Traces of Inuit temporary
stays there and ancient Thule sites.

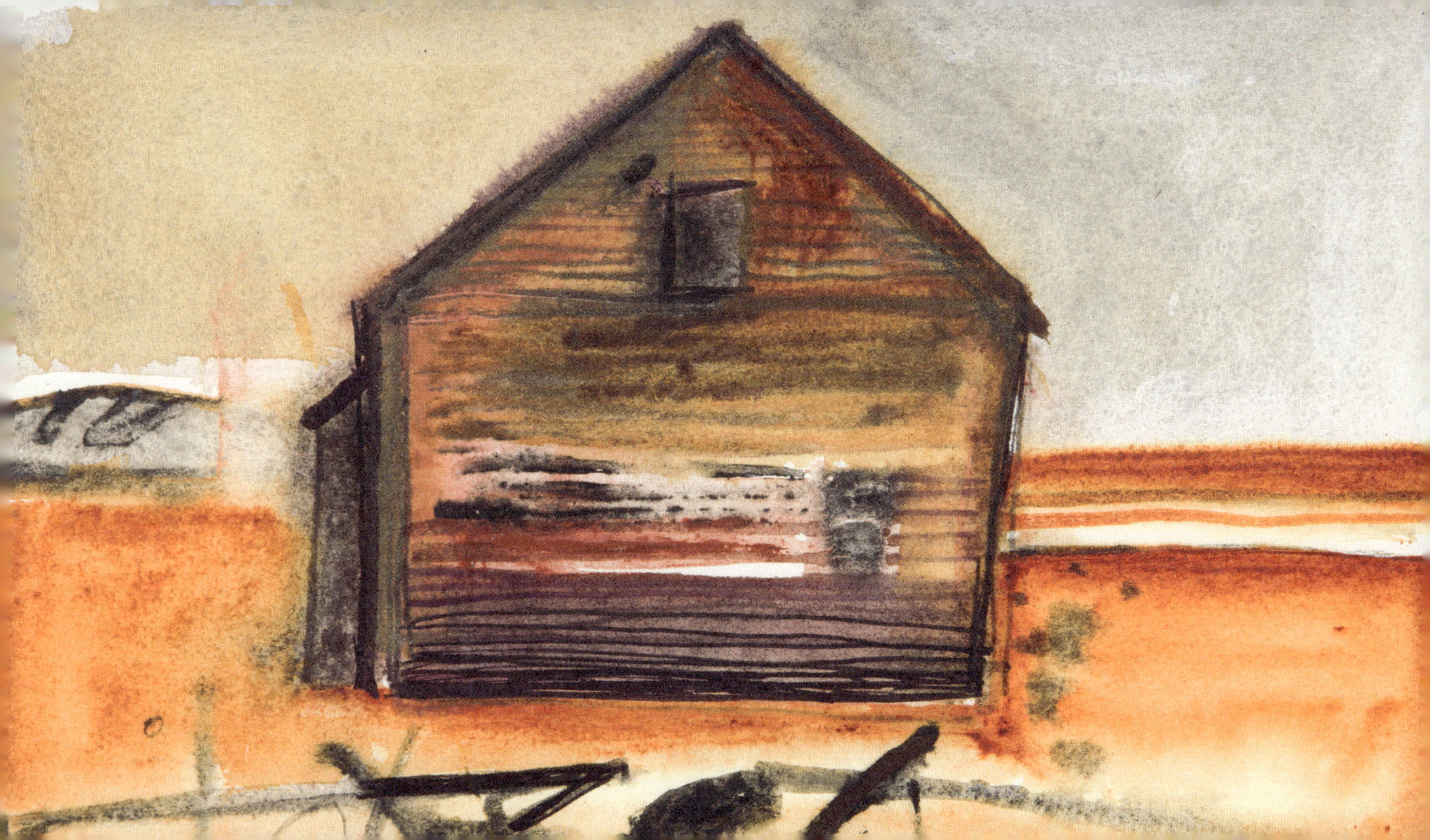

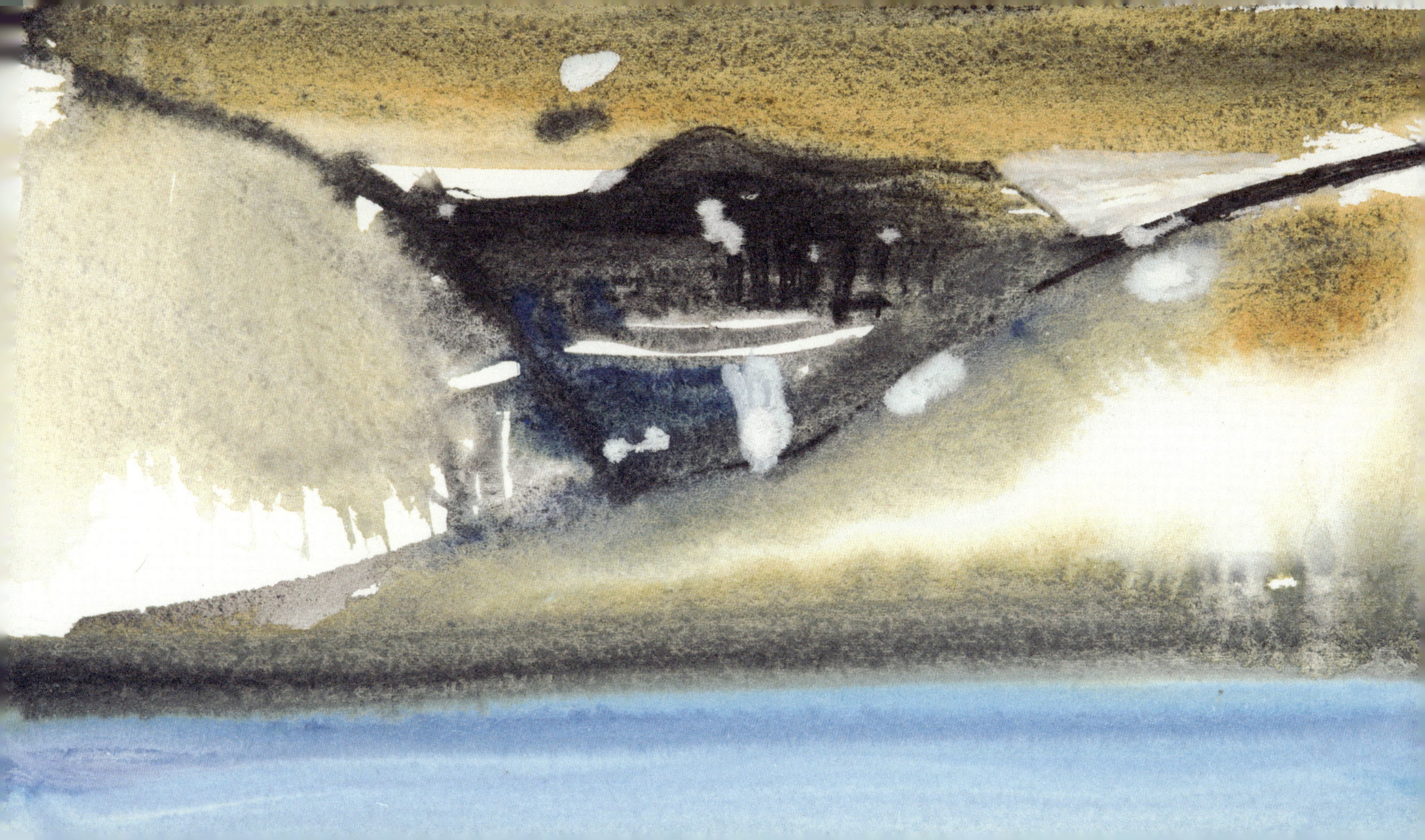

Fort Ross - Hudsons Bay site
Beautiful calm day.
Walked around the site looking at fragments of the past, bones, bits of rusty tin, enamel lids, all integrated into the colourful arctic tundra. Vivid colours of the moss, small flowers and lichen. Even small mushrooms.
The huts had deteriorated since last year.
Too many people visiting the site, shifting bones and taking souvenirs.
On this very pleasant day it is very hard to imagine what a bleak life the company people led there in the dead of a frozen winter.

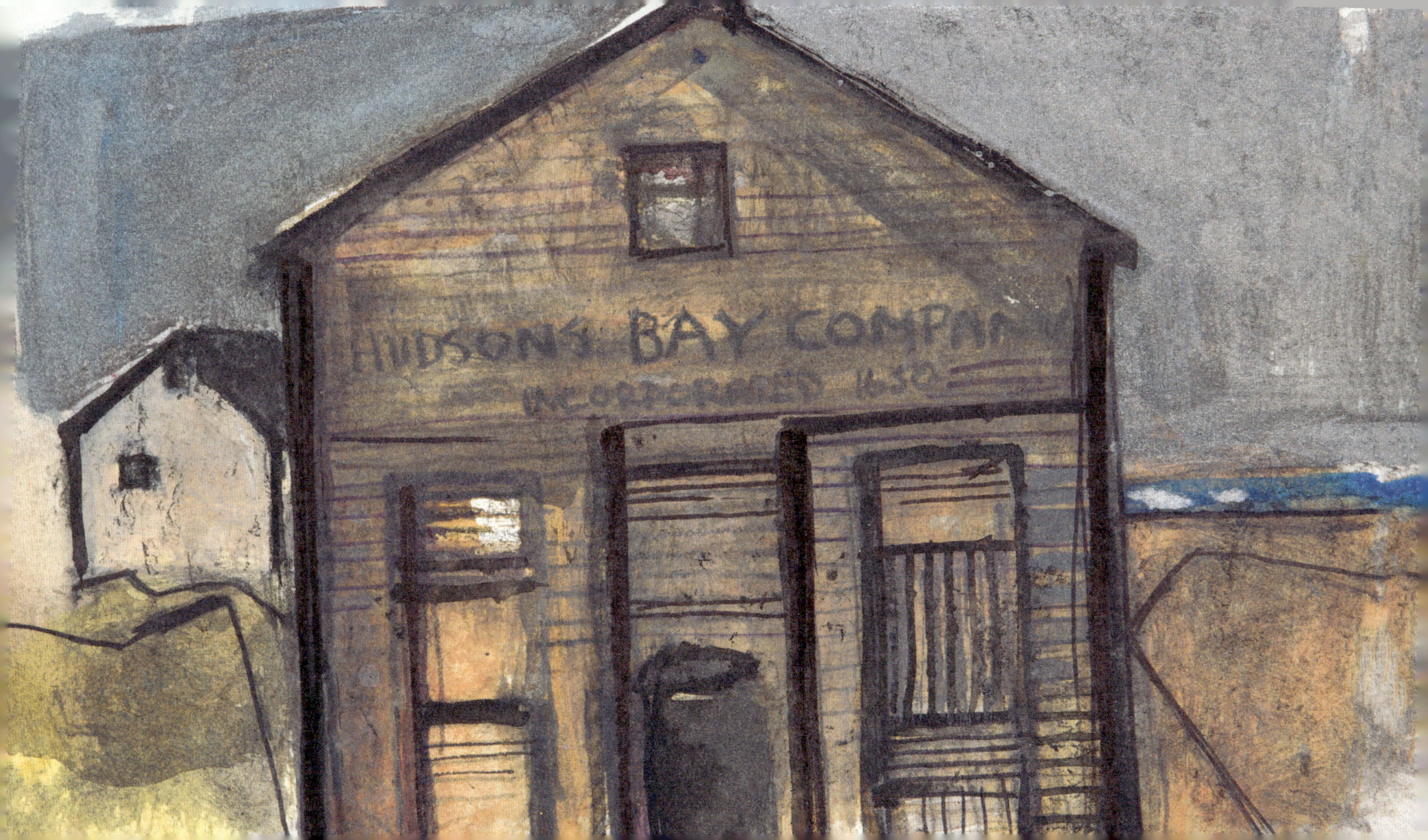
HUDSONS BAY COMPAN

Fort Ross – Visited by John Rae

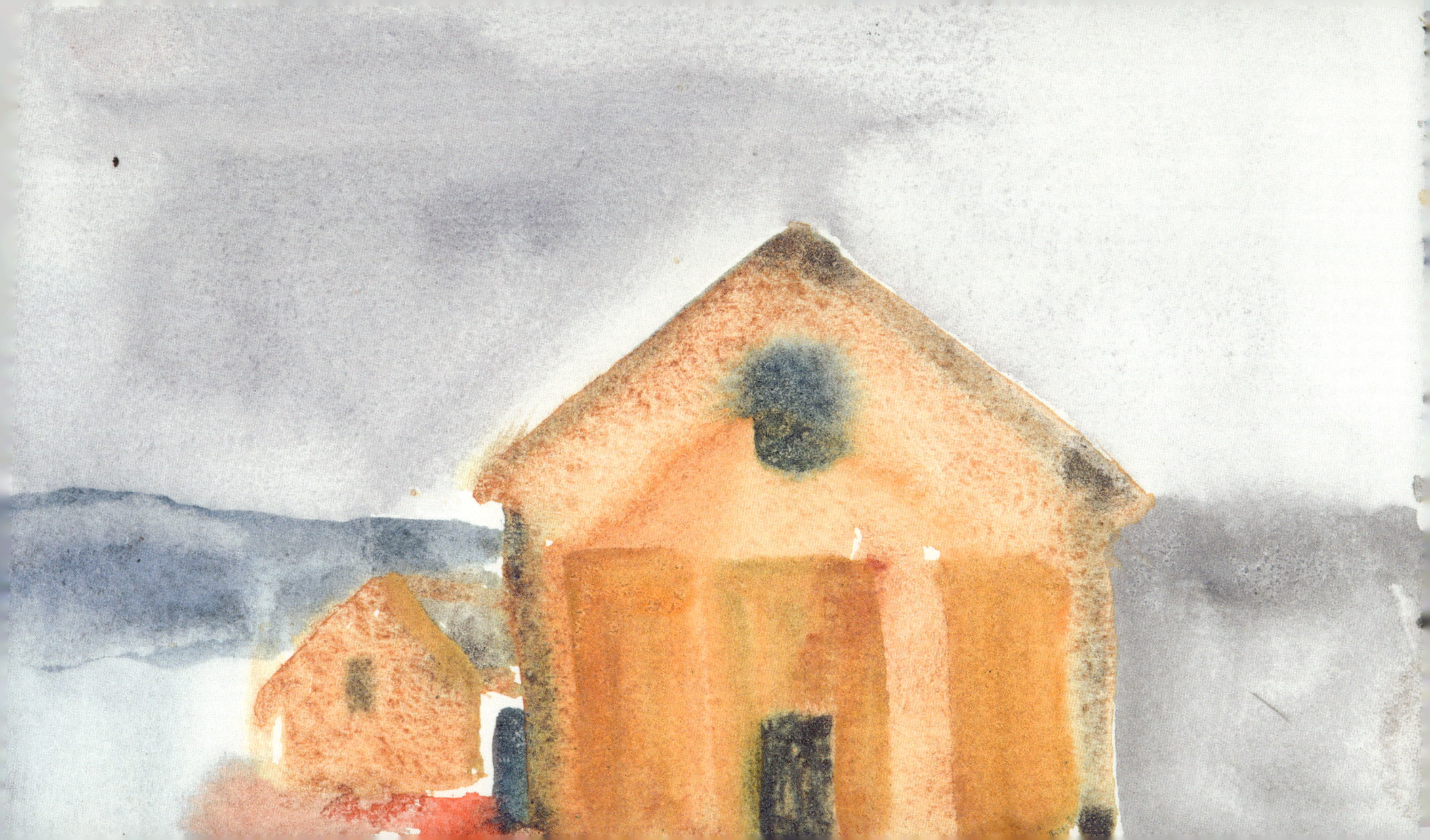

Bellot strait – cold but clear. Stiff wind
Dark, dramatic skies, black clouds
layered into the distance.
Some narwal spotted and a group of
seals otherwise nothing.
Not as dramatic as last year without
the beautiful sunset.

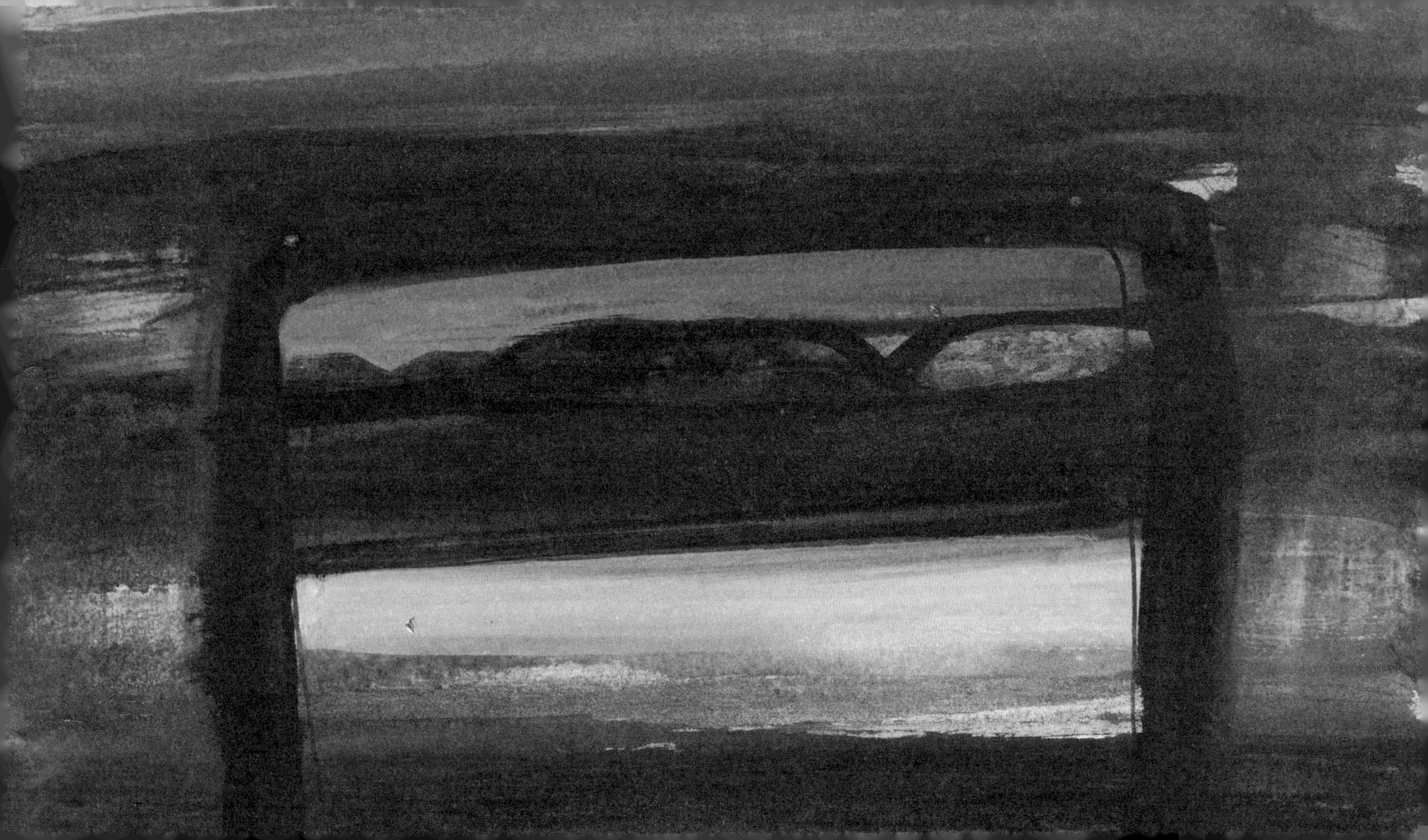

Cunningham Bay – Hope to see whales – dead or alive, and polar bears.
Waited all day at anchor before the wind finally dropped and we could go into the bay on the zodiacs. We saw 6/7 bears eating the beluga carcasses. Water too choppy to get any photos. Finally back at the ship frozen at 8pm.
Beautiful calm sunny evening

Polar brothers with Red Faces – eating Beluga carcas

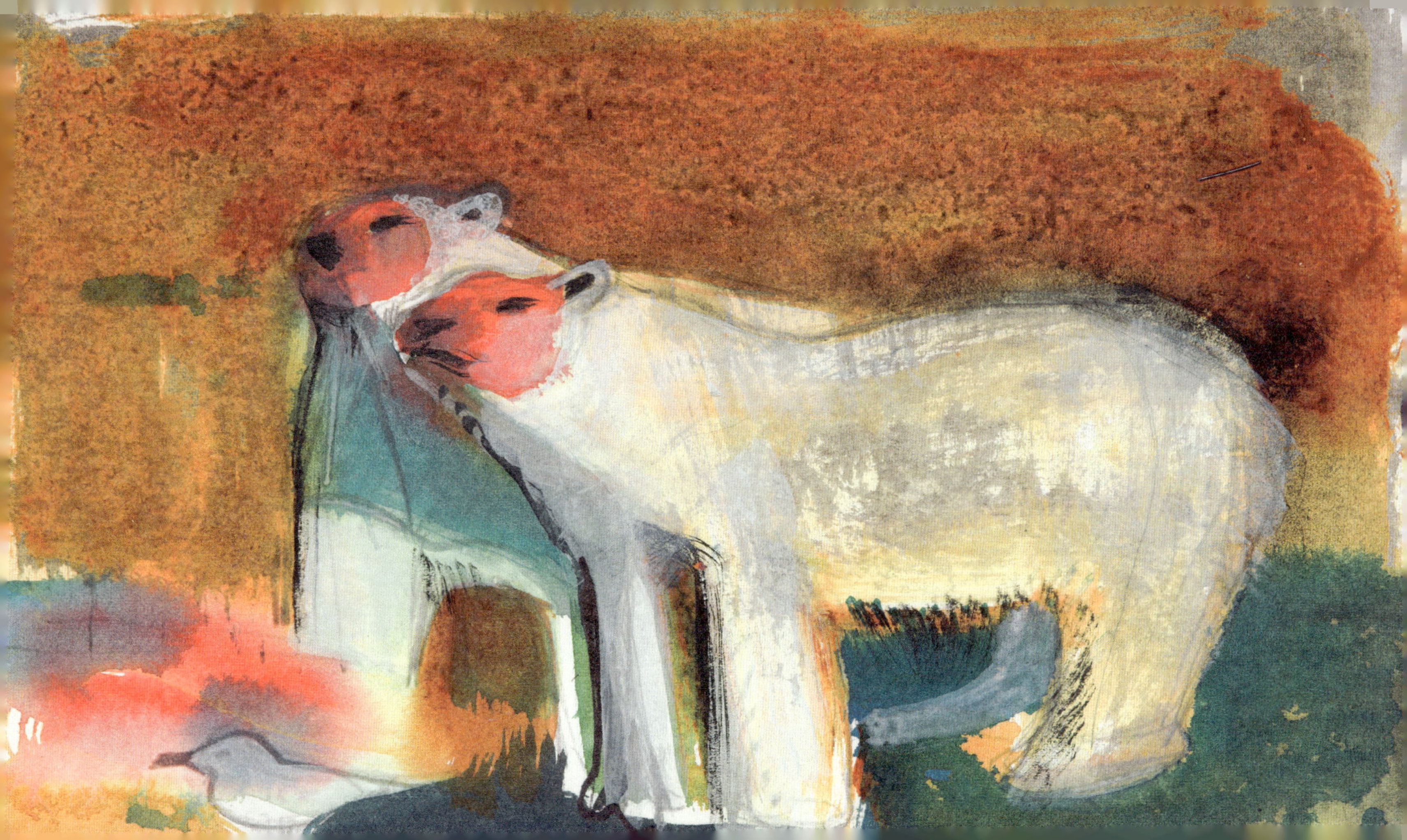

North West Passage - 2017

Edmonton - Resolute - Greenland

24 aug 2017

Boarded flight from Edmonton to Resolute Bay. Diverted from Cambridge Bay owing to Sea Ice.

Resolute, a desolute settlement of 200, Inuit plus support staff for the airporte. Inuit resettled here to cement Canada's claim to the North West Passage.

Moving from the berth here about 9 pm on route to Beechy Island tomorrow. Very unexpected to be seeing this so early in the voyage.

25 aug 2017 Sailing Past Somerset Island
Beautiful sunrise and ice flows. South on Peel Sound.

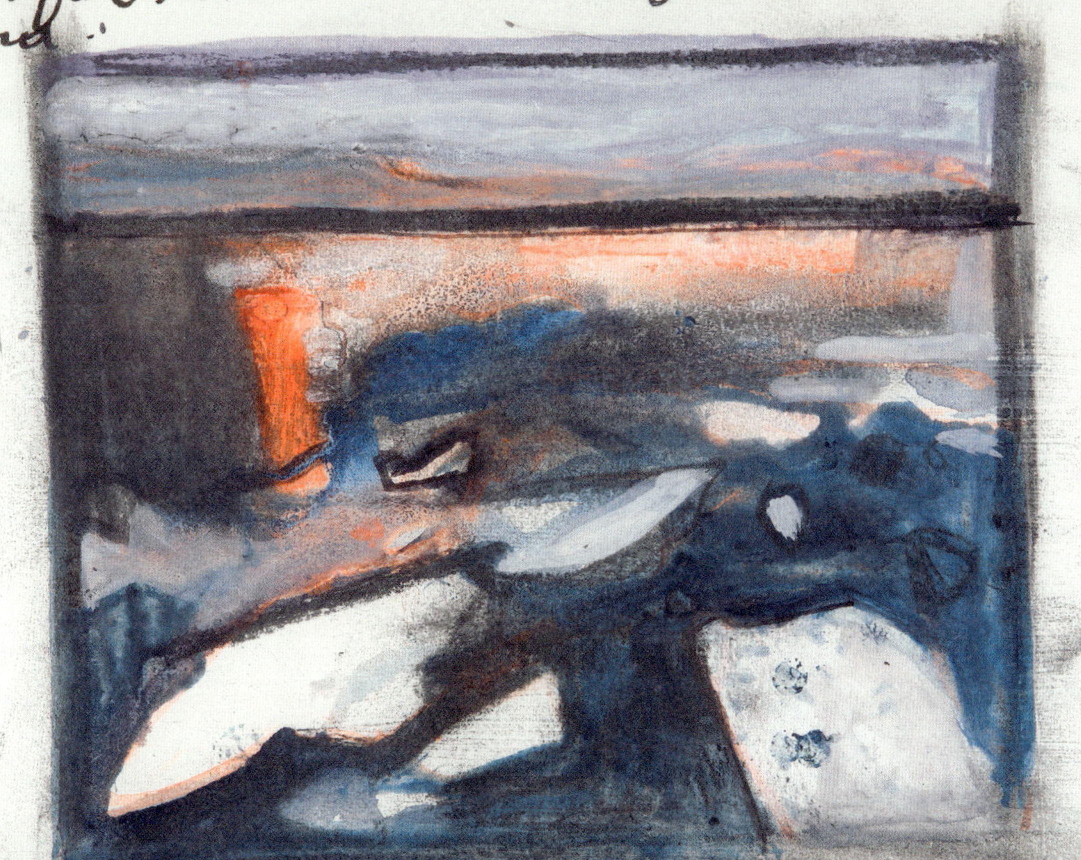

This morning saw 3 Polar Bears – close enough to get good photographs of them on the ice floes. This afternoon, a female and two cubs close enough to photograph. They took off into the water and the boat followed them for too long. Qiet afternoon while most passengers are off on a zodiac cruise to no where. 2 hours of beeing cold.

Sailing Down Peel Sound.

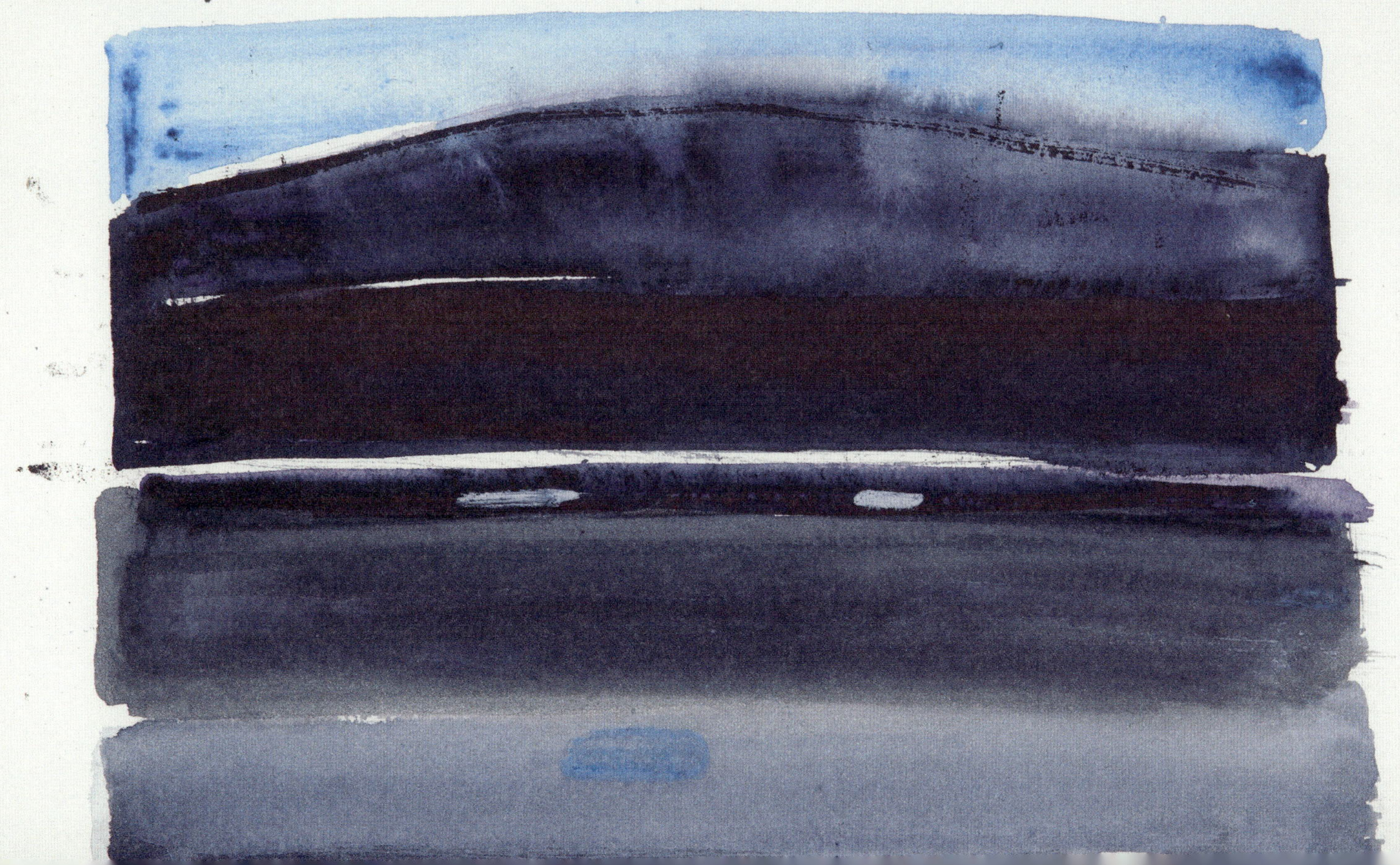

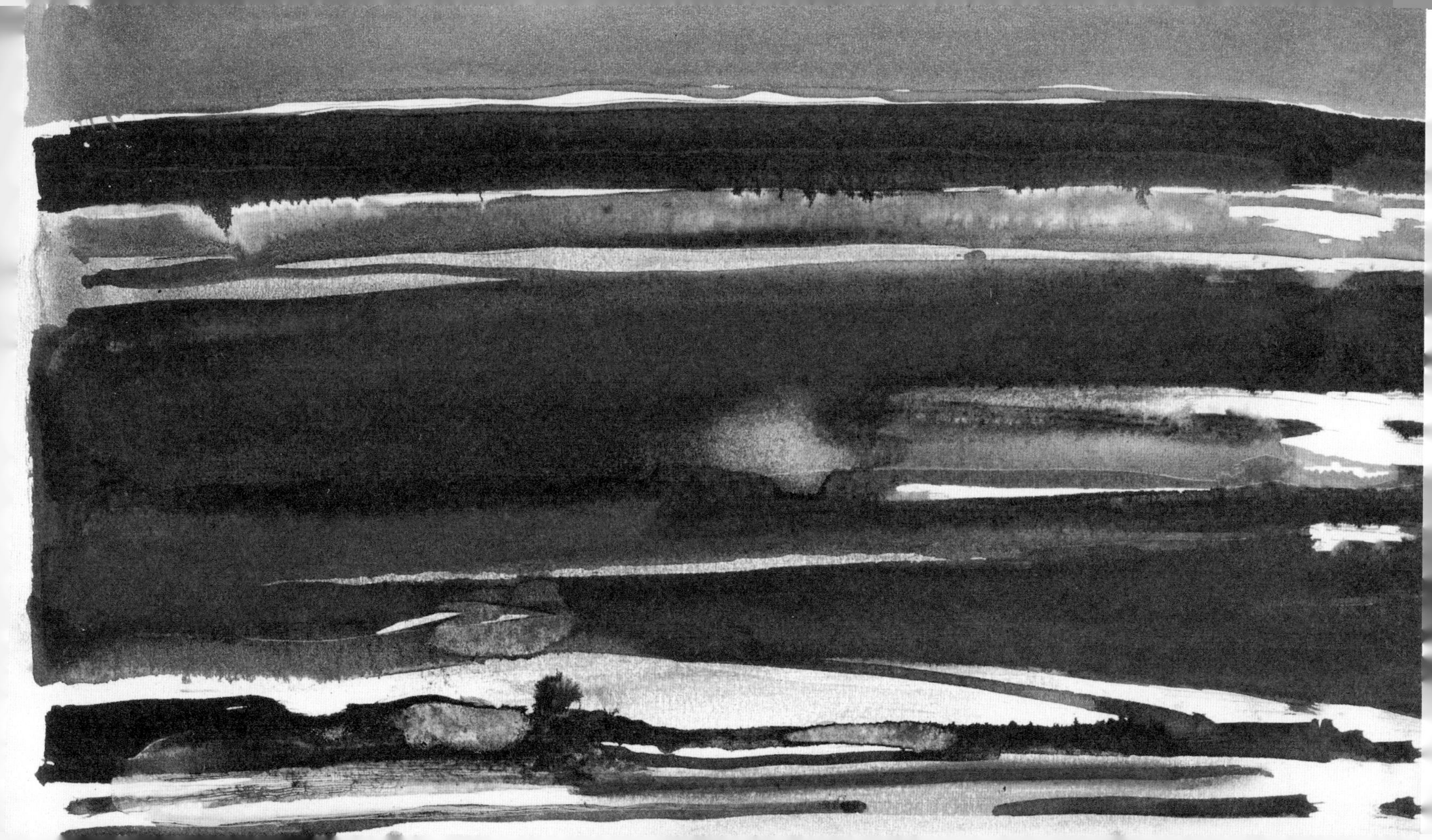

Bear - Peel Sound

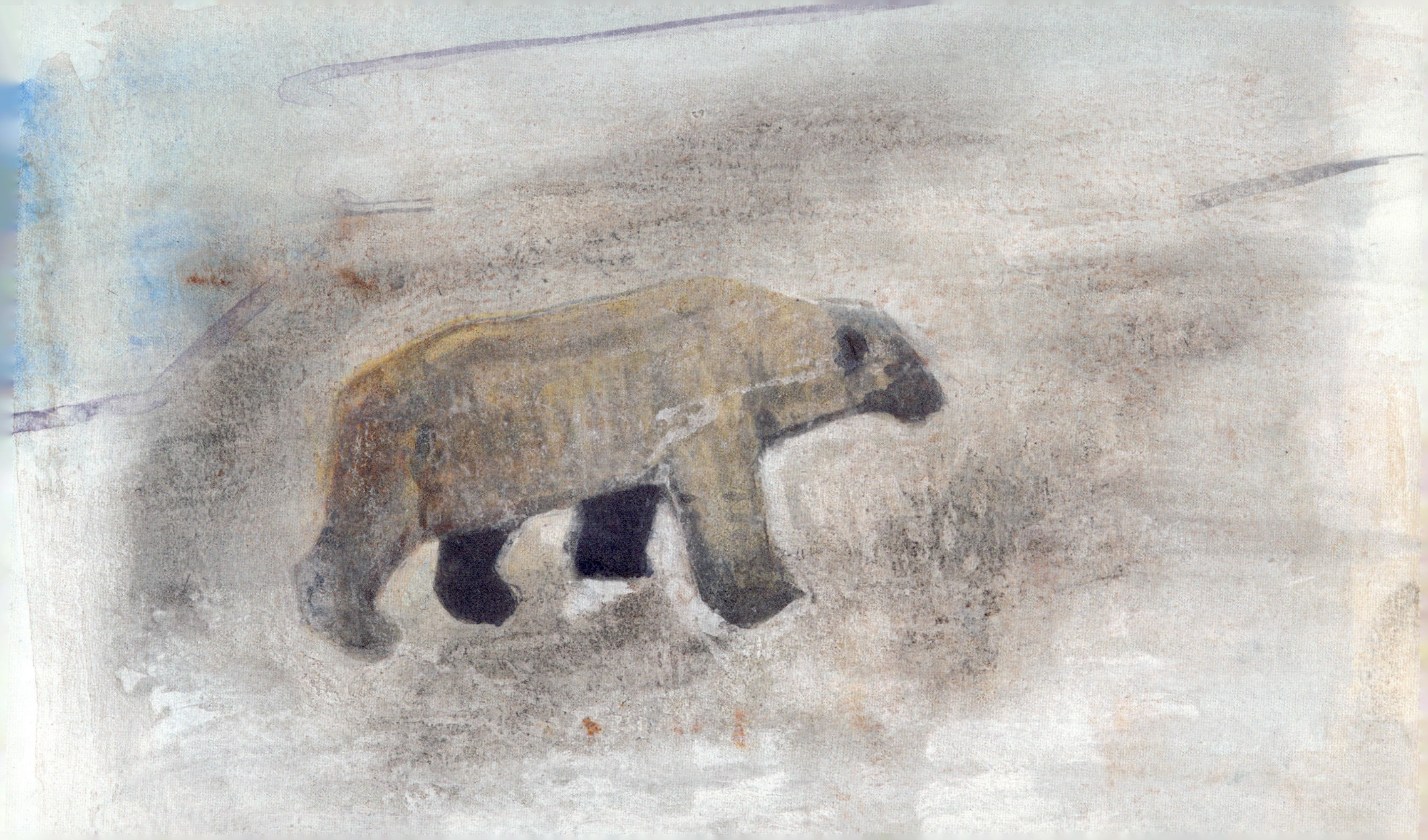

26 August Peel Sound - 4:30 AM
The ship is having difficulty getting through heavy ice. The visibility is poor - thick fog.

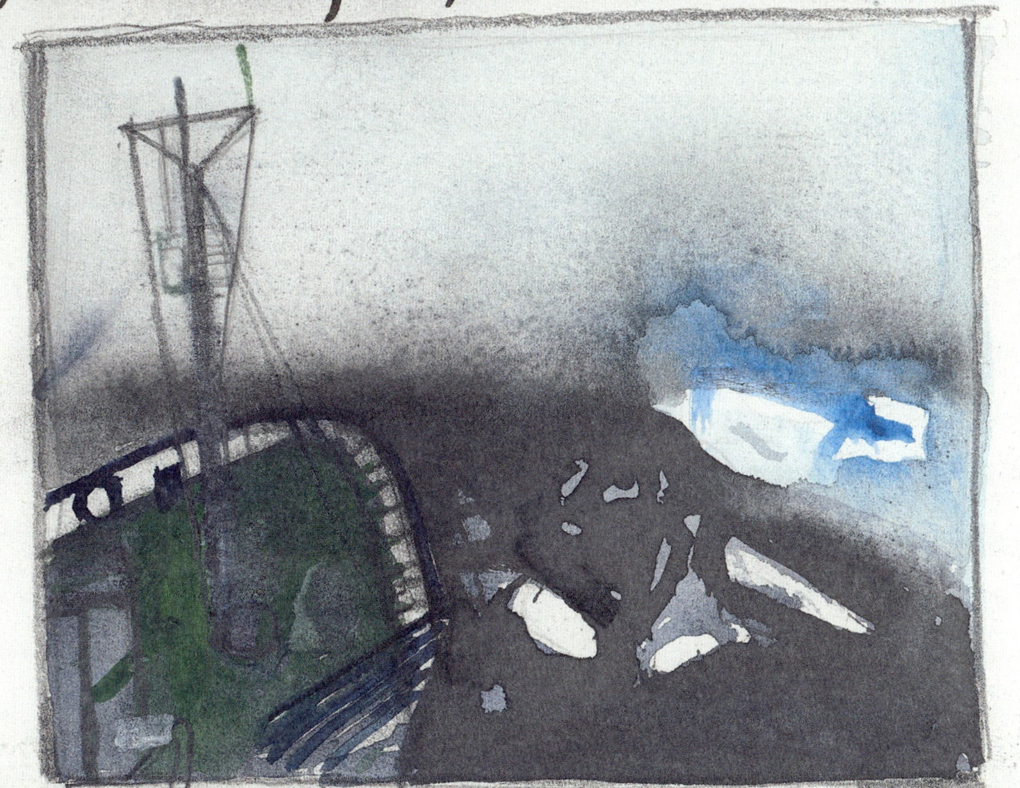

26 august – Waiting at the entrance to Bellot Strait. Very thick sea ice so the captain is waiting for the current to come from the east to break it up. That will be a wait of three hours. Maybe we will have to go back up Peel Sound – north to Beechey.

27 Aug. Outside Bellot Strait. Sea ice preventing passage, so awaiting ice breaker to cut through to strait. Amazing sunset and now dark twilight with ice floes. Mesmerising.

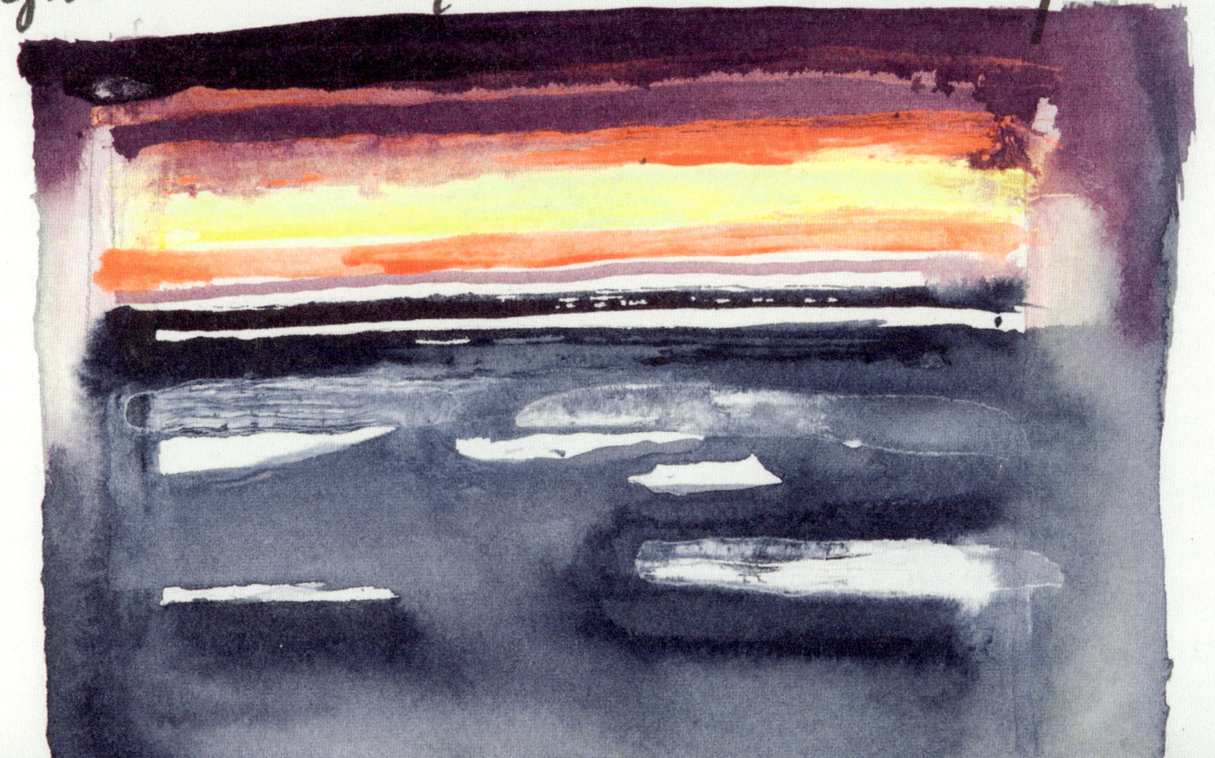

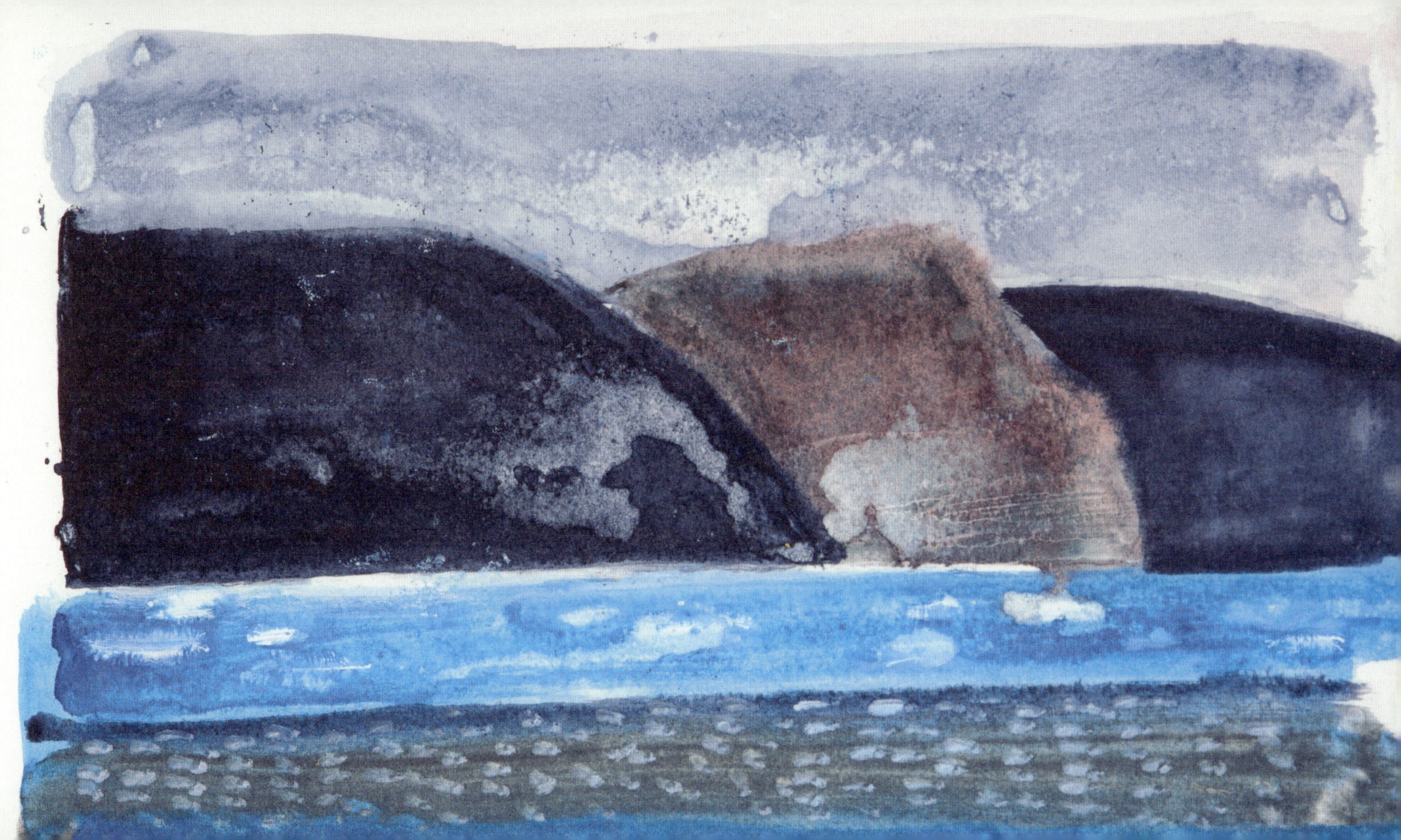

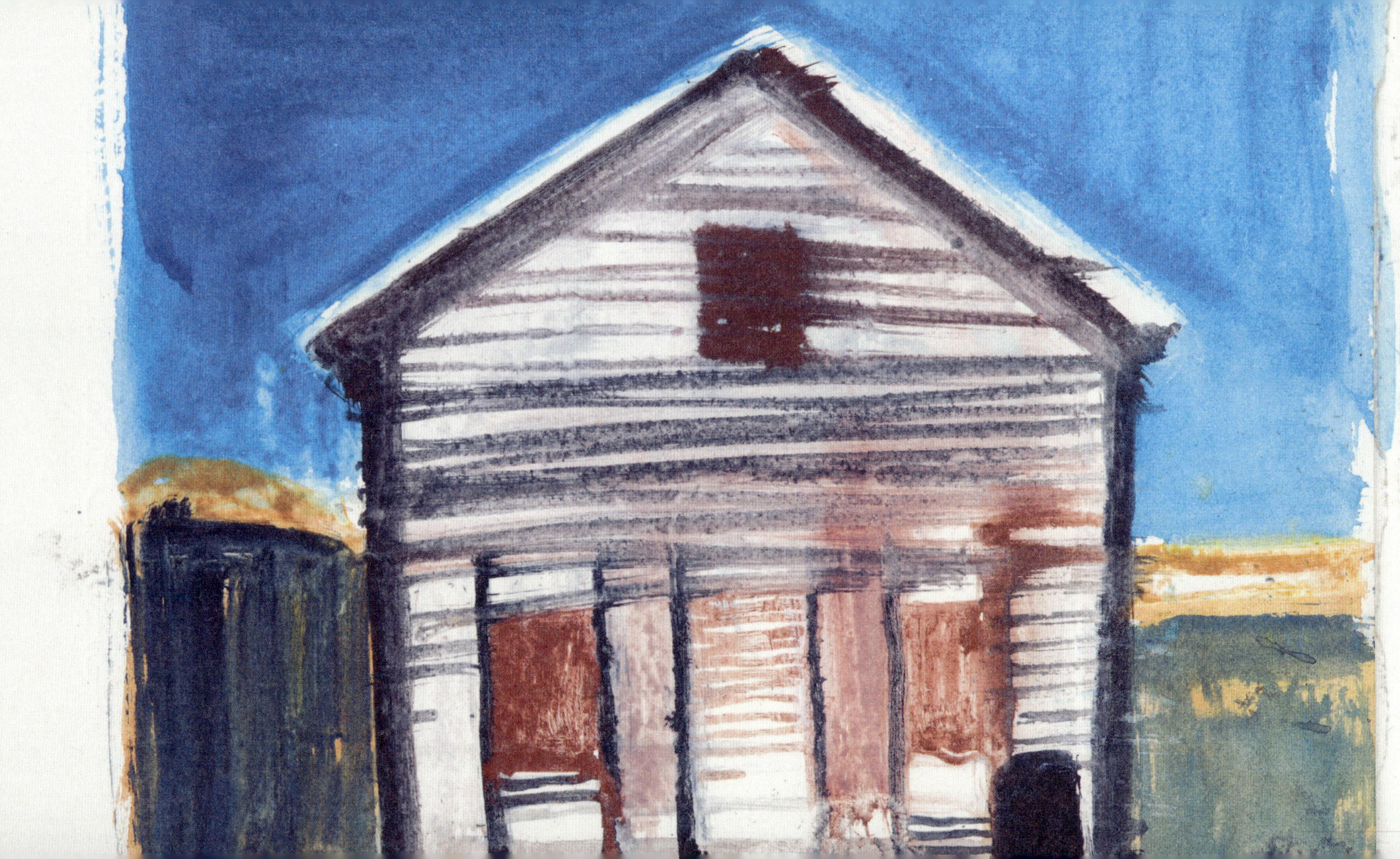

8 aug afternoon HBC Huts at Fort Ross.

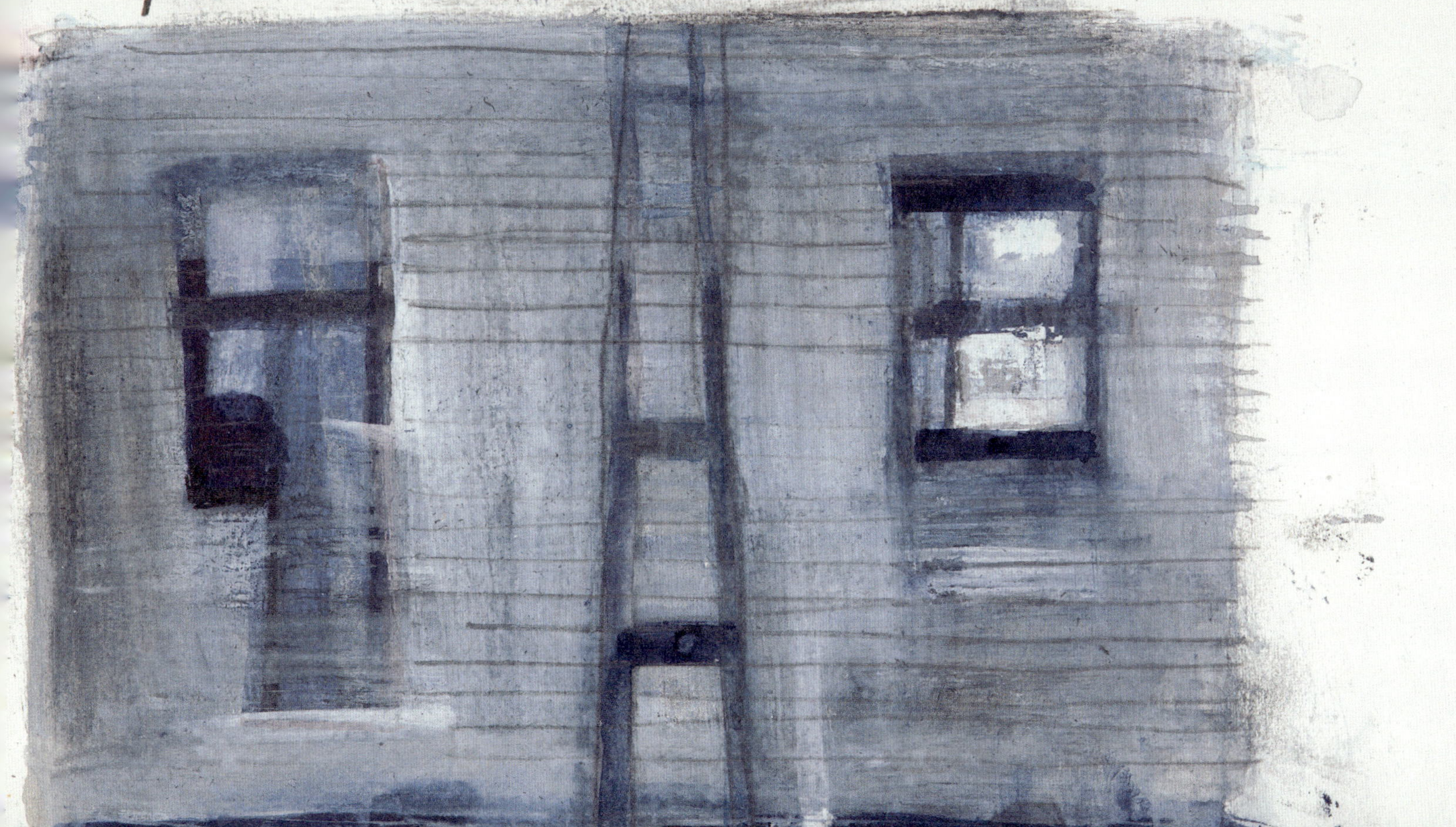

29 Aug – Beechey Island grave site.

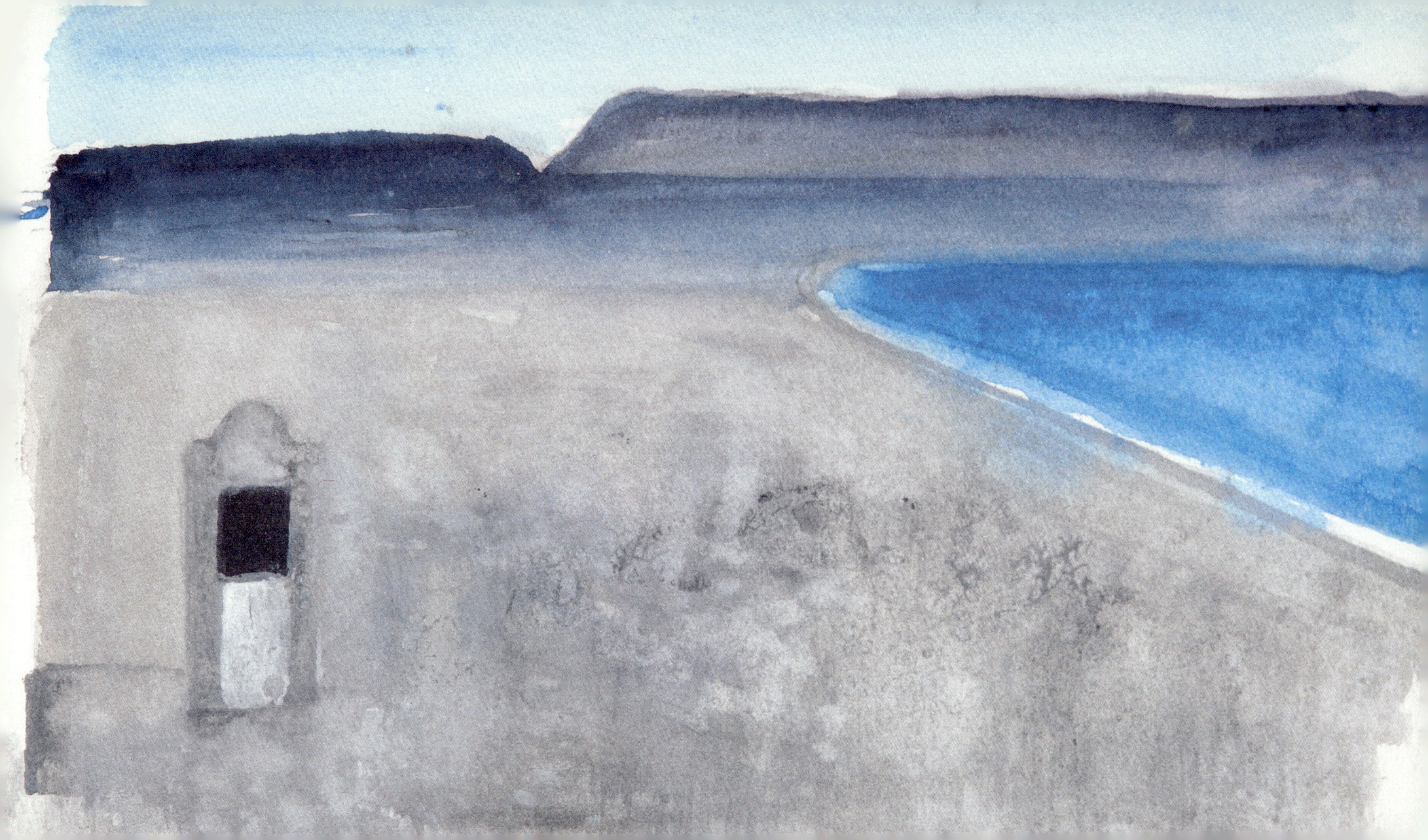

30 aug. Croker Glacier – Sailed into Croker Bay
calm water with small bergs and broken ice.
Sailed right up to the glacier. Amazing colour
a walrus with pup was spotted but I failed to be
in the right place to see it.

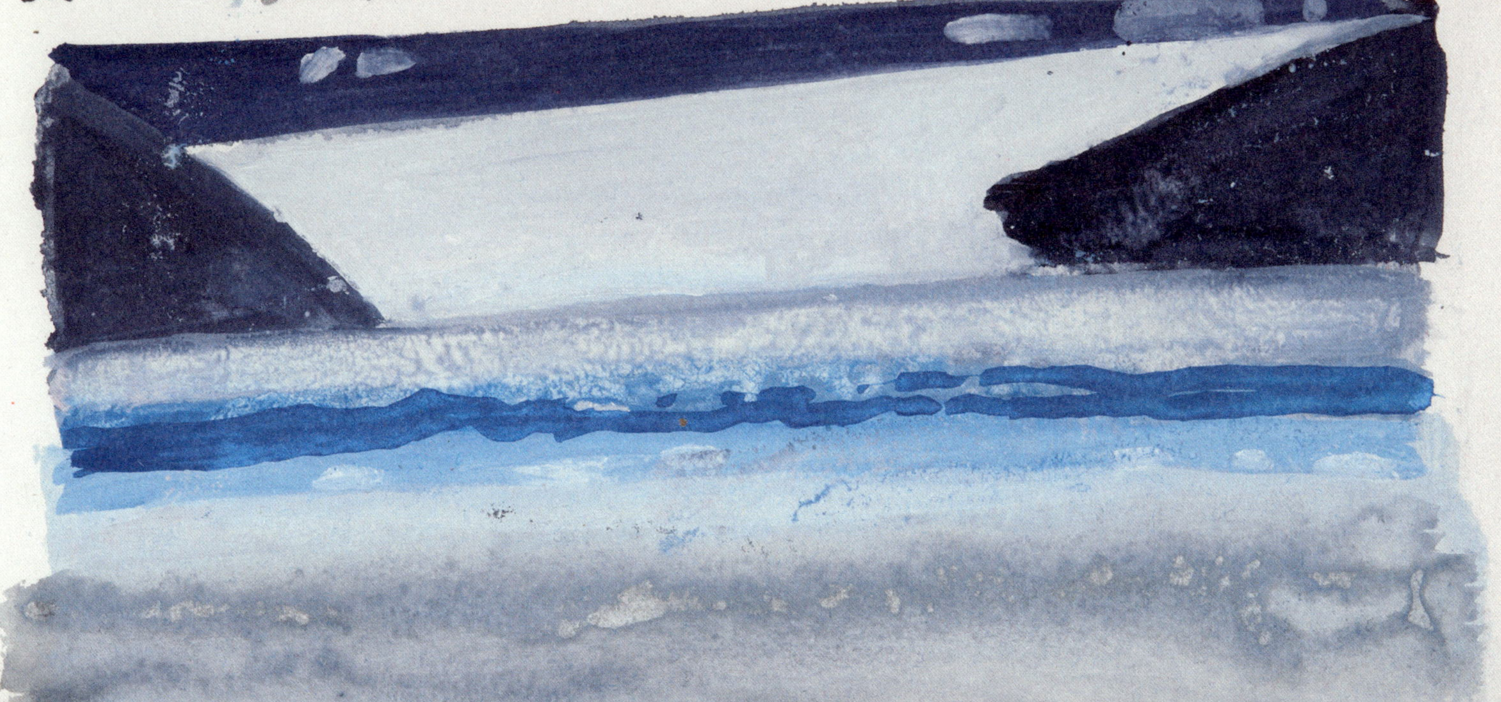

30 aug. Dundas Harbour. RCMP Post.
Thule sites – many animal bones and skulls
The hut site has about 5 structures of wood in
various states of disintegration. Too many red
coated people on site to fully appreciate its ..
desolation.

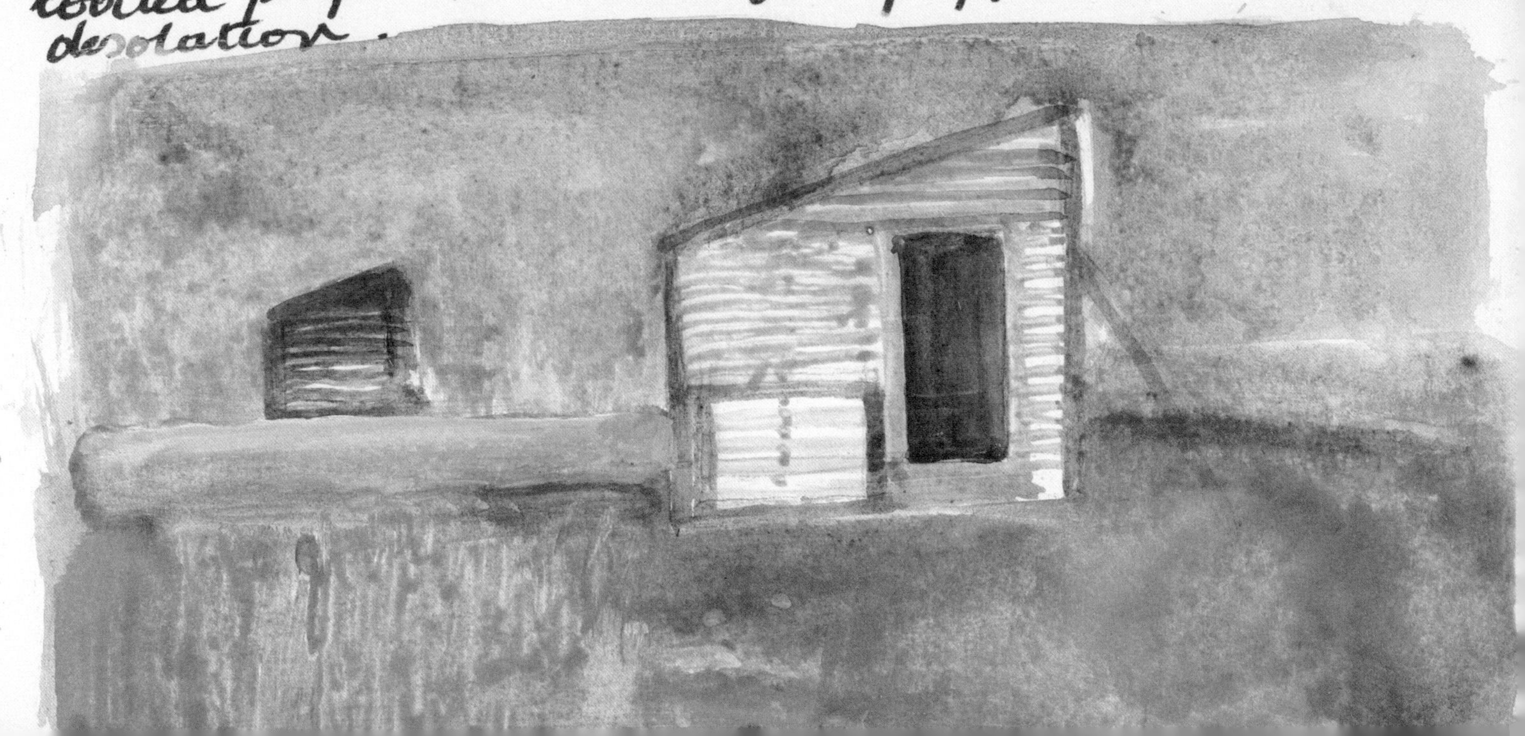

31 Aug – Pond Inlet – Lovely Day, mild and calm
Wearing too many clothes. Vistided the community
centre to watch the Inuit presentation. Much better
than 2015 but still no good craft. work for sale
They need artists and craftspeople to come in to
inrigorate the creativity of the community.

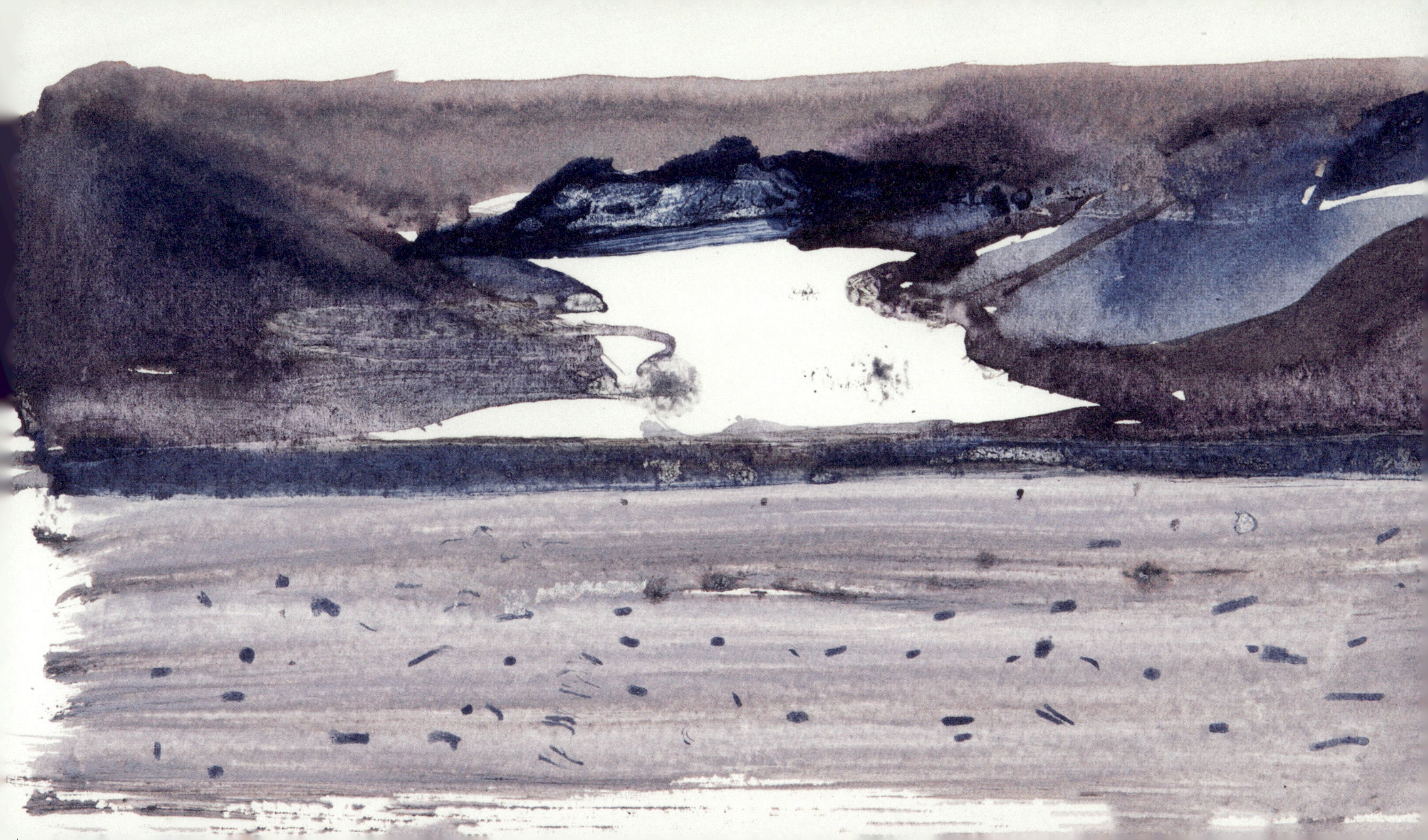

1 Sept Gibbs Fiord, a long beautiful inlet on Baffin Island. Hanging glaciers and majestic towering cliffs. Blue green water. There is a landing but as it looks like mostly shale, I will give it a miss.

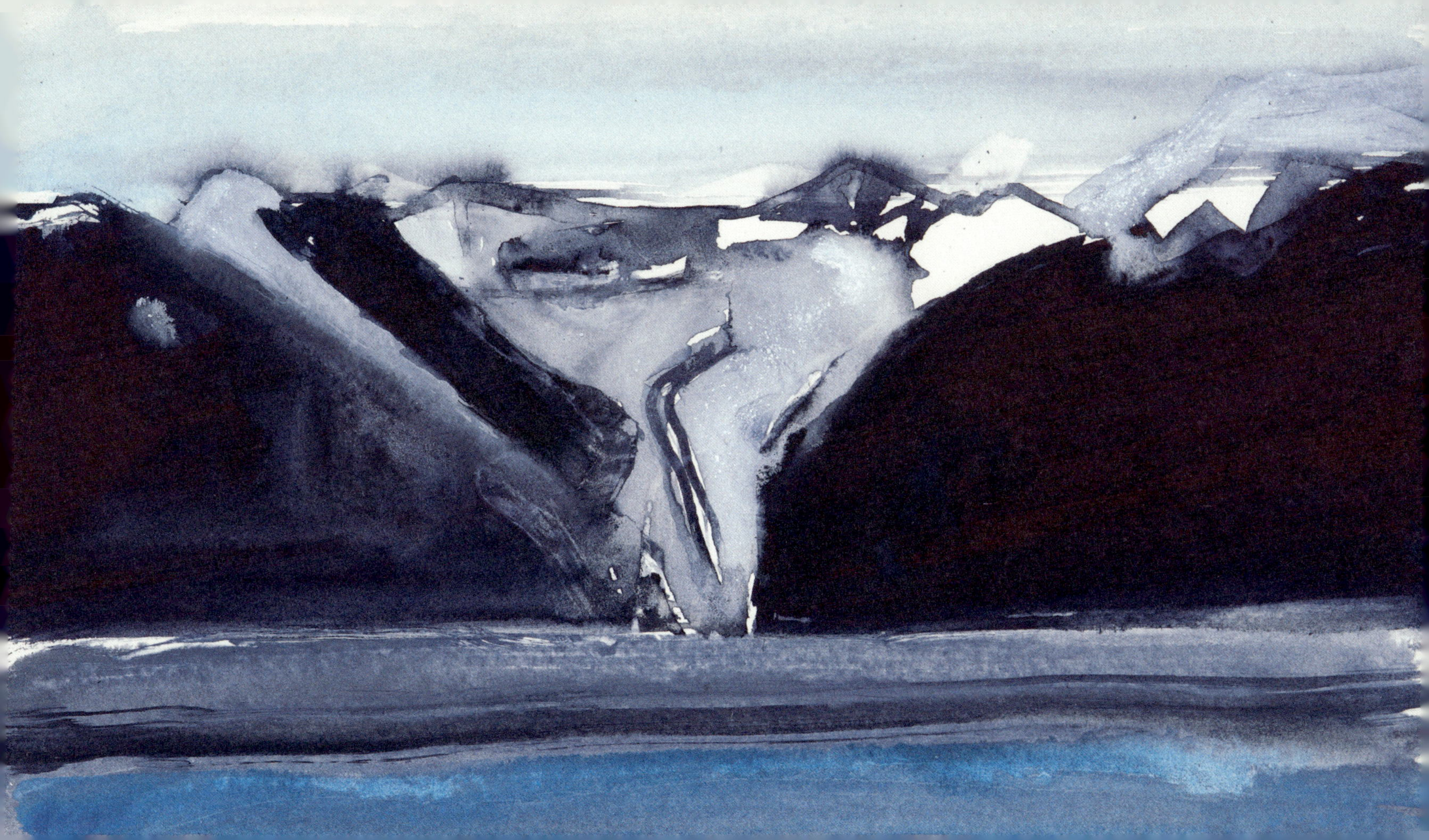

2 Sept – Sailed down Baffin Island to Isabella Bay. The sea is calm with no wind – a wonderful sunrise and a few Icebergs. We will be looking for bowhead whales this morning.

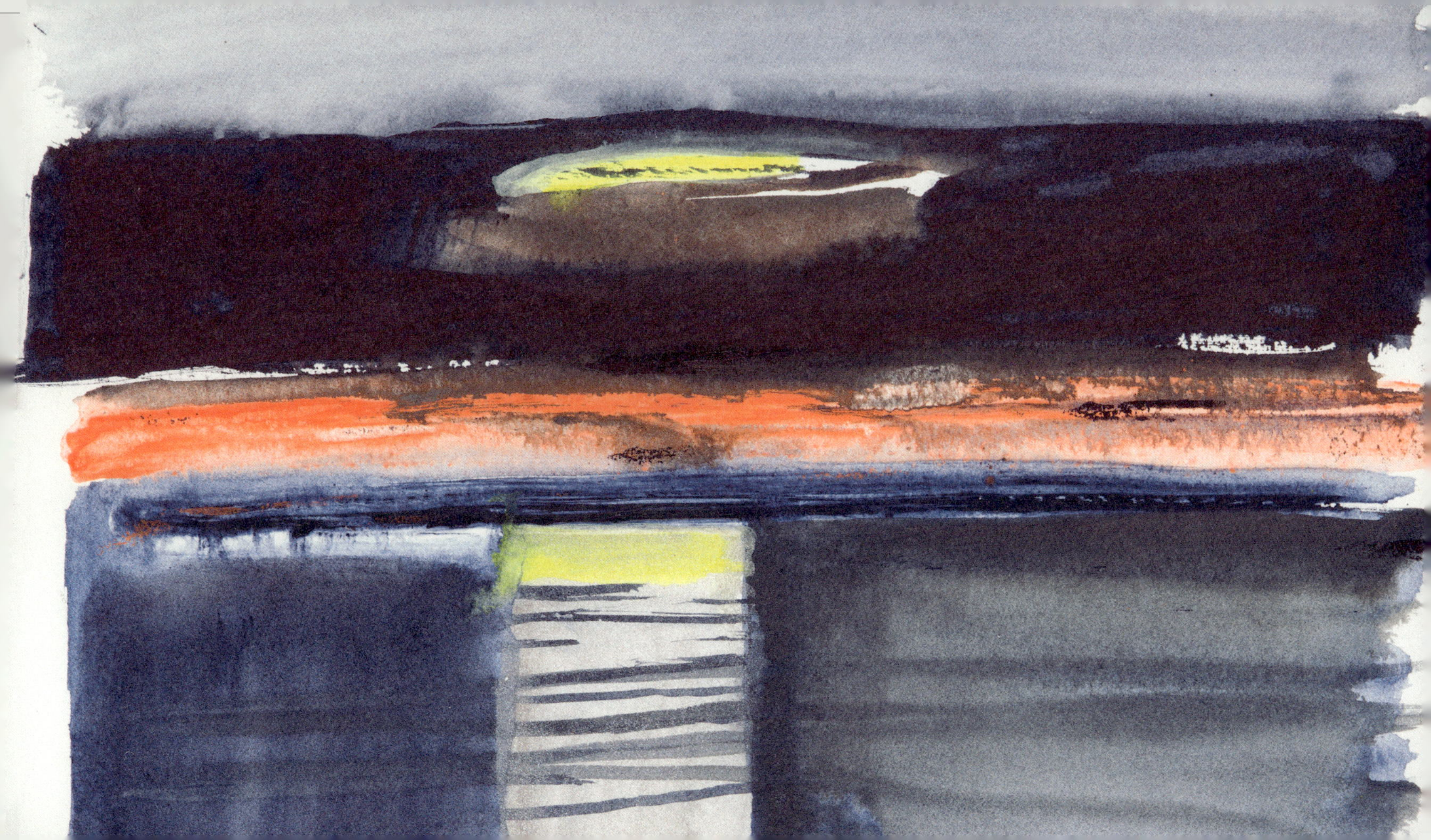

2 Sept 2017 Isabella Bay. Whale watching
Saw some black dots but none close enough!

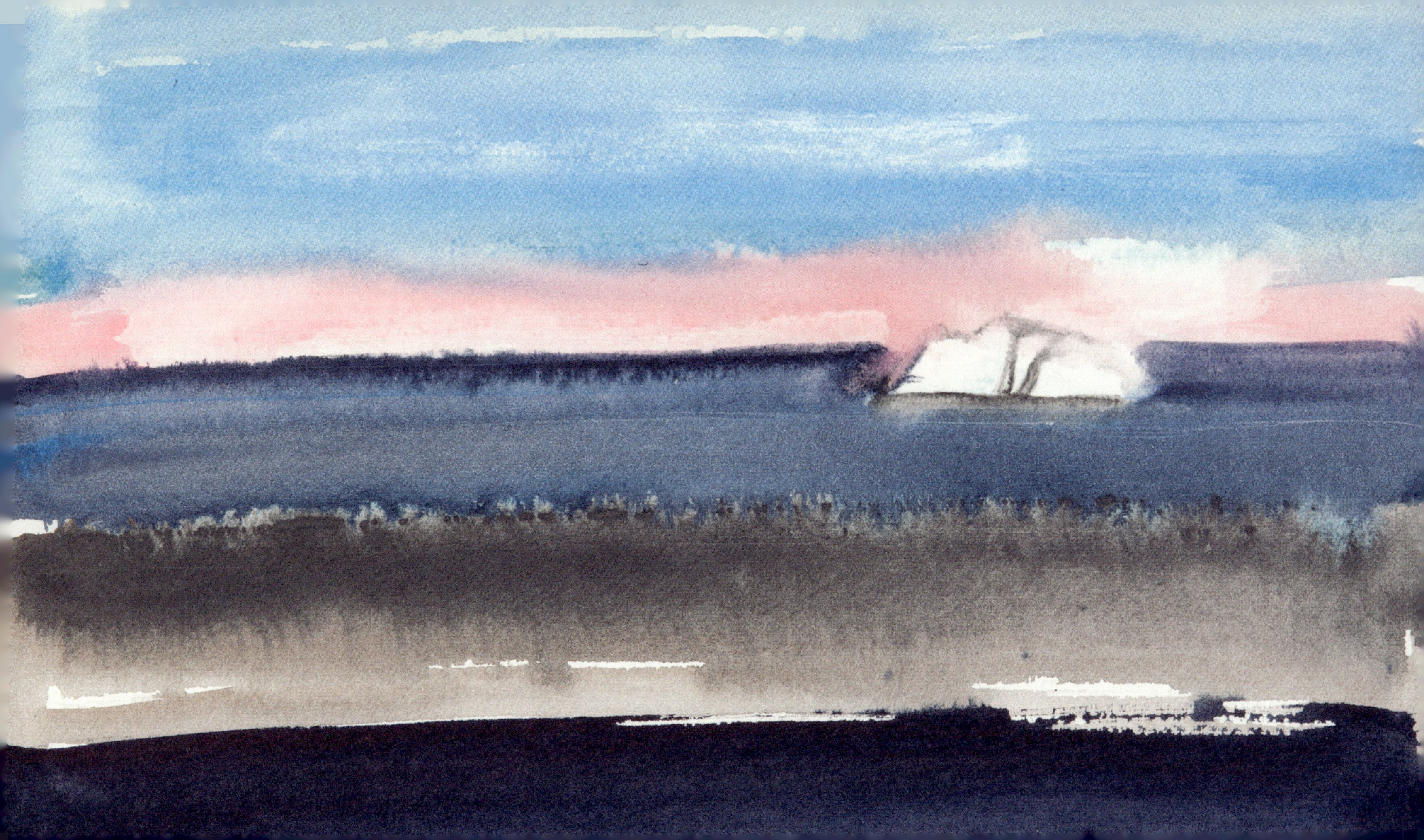

a day sailing across Davis Strait. Nothing to see except occasional small ice bergs.
4 Sept – sailing into Ilulissat – I can see ice at the mouth of the glacier but no dramatic large. bergs so far.
Arrived early at Ilulissat and hired a small plane for a flight over the ice cap and Jacobshaven glacier. absolutely spectacular. Massive fast moving ice sheet – 40 K per day. World Heritage site. Flew out over the ice bergs at the edge of the glacier and saw two groups of whales. The afternoon was spent in the zodiacs cruising through the ice bergs. Luckily a beautiful calm afternoon. We are now sailing towards Sisimiut on a calm morning with a perfectly clear sky and a golden sunrise.

The sketchbooks reproduced here were used by Barbara Rae during three journeys to the Arctic in August 2015, August 2016 and August 2017.

Royal Academy Publications
Florence Dassonville, Production Coordinator
Carola Krueger, Production Manager
Peter Sawbridge, Editorial Director
Nick Tite, Publisher

Design
Kathrin Jacobsen

Photography
Pages 3, 22–23, 72, 75, 79, 81–83, 85, 87–89, 92–94, 96–100, 102, 104, 106: Prudence Cuming Associates
All other images: Jed Gordon Creative

Printed in Wales by Gomer Press

British Library Cataloguing-in-Publication Data A catalogue record for this book is available from the British Library
ISBN 978-1-912520-11-4

Distributed outside the United States and Canada by ACC Art Books Ltd, Riverside House, Dock Lane, Melton, Woodbridge, Suffolk IP12 1PE

Distributed in the United States and Canada by ARTBOOK | D.A.P., 155 Sixth Avenue, New York NY 10013